BASEBALL CARDS

Text by
Bill Shannon

PRICE STERN SLOAN
Los Angeles

Officially licensed by Major League Baseball

Official Licensee

© 1988 MLBPA
© MSA

An MBKA Production

Printed and bound in Hong Kong .

TEAM LEADERS

Hall of Famers
Grover Alexander
Cap Anson
Ernie Banks
Lou Boudreau (Manager)
Roger Bresnahan
Lou Brock
Mordecai Brown
Frank Chance
John Clarkson
Kiki Cuyler
Dizzy Dean
Hugh Duffy
Johnny Evers
Jimmie Foxx
Frankie Frisch (Manager)
Clark Griffith
Burleigh Grimes
Gabby Hartnett
Billy Herman
Rogers Hornsby
Monte Irvin
George Kelly
Mike "King" Kelly
Ralph Kiner
Chuck Klein
Fred Lindstrom
Rabbit Maranville
Joe McCarthy (Manager)
Robin Roberts
A.G. Spalding
Joe Tinker
Rube Waddell
Hoyt Wilhelm
Billy Williams
Hack Wilson

No-Hitters
(Since 1901)
6-11-04 Bob Wicker (at New York)
7-31-10 King Cole (at St. Louis)
8-31-15 Jim Lavender
    (at New York)
5-02-17 Hippo Vaughn (vs. Reds)
5-12-55 Sam Jones (vs. Pirates)
5-15-60 Don Cardwell
    (vs. Cardinals)
8-19-69 Ken Holtzman
    (vs. Braves)
6-03-71 Ken Holtzman
    (at Cincinnati)
4-16-72 Burt Hooton (vs. Phillies)
9-02-72 Milt Pappas (vs. Padres)

Twenty-Game Winners
(Since 1901)
1902 - Jack Taylor (22)
1903 - Jack Taylor (21)
    Jake Weimer (20)
    Bob Wicker (20)
1904 - Jake Weimer (20)
1906 - Mordecai Brown (26)
    Jack Pfiester (20)
    *Jack Taylor (20)
1907 - Orval Overall (23)
    Mordecai Brown (20)
1908 - Mordecai Brown (29)
    Ed Reulbach (24)
1909 - Mordecai Brown (27)
    Orval Overall (20)
1910 - Mordecai Brown (25)
    King Cole (20)
1911 - Mordecai Brown (21)

1912 - Larry Cheney (26)
1913 - Larry Cheney (21)
1914 - Hippo Vaughn (21)
    Larry Cheney (20)
1915 - Hippo Vaughn (20)
1917 - Hippo Vaughn (23)
1918 - Hippo Vaughn (22)
1919 - Hippo Vaughn (21)
1920 - Grover Alexander (27)
1923 - Grover Alexander (22)
1927 - Charlie Root (26)
1929 - Pat Malone (22)
1930 - Pat Malone (20)
1932 - Lon Warneke (22)
1933 - Guy Bush (20)
1934 - Lon Warneke (22)
1935 - Bill Lee (20)
    Lon Warneke (20)
1938 - Bill Lee (22)
1940 - Claude Passeau (20)
1945 - Hank Wyse (22)
    **Hank Borowy (21)
1963 - Dick Ellsworth (22)
1964 - Larry Jackson (24)
1967 - Fergie Jenkins (20)
1968 - Fergie Jenkins (20)
1969 - Fergie Jenkins (21)
    Bill Hands (20)
1970 - Fergie Jenkins (22)
1971 - Fergie Jenkins (24)
1972 - Fergie Jenkins (20)
1977 - Rick Reuschel (20)
***1984 - Rick Sutcliffe (20)

*Pitched with Cardinals (8)
  and Cubs (12).
**Pitched with Yankees (10)
  and Cubs (11).
***Pitched with Indians (4) and
  Cubs (16).

League Leaders

Batting Average
1912 - Heinie Zimmerman (.372)
1945 - Phil Cavarretta (.355)
1972 - Billy Williams (.333)
1975 - Bill Madlock (.354)
1976 - Bill Madlock (.339)
1980 - Bill Buckner (.324)

Home Runs

*1910 - Frank Schulte (10)
1911 - Frank Schulte (21)
1912 - Heinie Zimmerman (14)
*1916 - Cy Williams (12)
1926 - Hack Wilson (21)
*1927 - Hack Wilson (30)
*1928 - Hack Wilson (31)
1930 - Hack Wilson (56)
1943 - Bill Nicholson (29)
1944 - Bill Nicholson (33)
*1952 - Hank Sauer (37)
1958 - Ernie Banks (47)
1960 - Ernie Banks (41)
1979 - Dave Kingman (48)
1987 - Andre Dawson (49)

*Tied

Runs Batting In

*1906 - Harry Steinfeldt (83)
1911 - Frank Schulte (121)
1912 - Heinie Zimmerman (98)
1918 - Fred Merkle (71)
1929 - Hack Wilson (159)
1930 - Hack Wilson (190)
1943 - Bill Nicholson (128)
1944 - Bill Nicholson (122)
1952 - Hank Sauer (121)
1958 - Ernie Banks (129)
1959 - Ernie Banks (143)
1987 - Andre Dawson (137)

*Tied

Wins

1909 - Mordecai Brown (27)
1912 - Larry Cheney (26)
1918 - Hippo Vaughn (22)
1920 - Grover Alexander (27)
1927 - Charlie Root (26)
1929 - Pat Malone (22)
*1930 - Pat Malone (20)

1932 - Lon Warneke (22)
1938 - Bill Lee (22)
1964 - Larry Jackson (24)
1971 - Fergie Jenkins (24)
1987 - Rick Sutcliffe (18)

*Tied

Strikeouts

*1906 - Fred Beebe (171)
1909 - Orval Overall (205)
1918 - Hippo Vaughn (148)
1919 - Hippo Vaughn (141)
1920 - Grover Alexander (173)
1929 - Pat Malone (166)
1938 - Clay Bryant (135)
*1939 - Claude Passeau (137)
**1946 - Johnny Schmitz (135)
1955 - Sam Jones (198)
1956 - Sam Jones (176)
1969 - Fergie Jenkins (273)

*Pitched with Cubs (55) and Cardinals (116).
**Tied for lead while pitching with Phillies (29) and Cubs (108).

Earned Run Average

1918 - Hippo Vaughn (1.74)
1919 - Grover Alexander (1.72)
1920 - Grover Alexander (1.91)
1932 - Lon Warneke (2.37)
1938 - Bill Lee (2.66)
1945 - Hank Borowy (2.14)

Most Valuable Players

1911 - Frank Schulte
1929 - Rogers Hornsby
1935 - Gabby Hartnett
1945 - Phil Cavarretta
1952 - Hank Sauer
1958 - Ernie Banks
1959 - Ernie Banks
1984 - Ryne Sandberg
1987 - Andre Dawson

Rookies of the Year

1961 - Billy Williams
1962 - Ken Hubbs

Cy Young Award Winners

1971 - Fergie Jenkins
1979 - Bruce Sutter
1984 - Rick Sutcliffe

World Series Appearances

1906	1918	1938
*1907	1929	1945
*1908	1932	
1910	1935	

*World Champions

Chicago Cubs Club Records (Since 1901)

Batting

Runs	Rogers Hornsby (156, 1929)
Hits	Rogers Hornsby (229, 1929)
Doubles	Billy Herman (57, 1935)
	Billy Herman (57, 1936)
Triples	Frank Schulte (21, 1911)
	Vic Saier (21, 1913)
Home Runs	Hack Wilson (56, 1930)
Runs Batted In	Hack Wilson (190, 1930)
Stolen Bases	Frank Chance (67, 1903)
Batting Average	Rogers Hornsby (.380, 1929)

Pitching

Games	Ted Abernathy (84, 1965)
	Dick Tidrow (84, 1980)
Innings	Grover Alexander (363.1, 1920)
Wins	Mordecai Brown (29, 1908)
Strikeouts	Fergie Jenkins (274, 1970)
Saves	Bruce Sutter (37, 1979)
Earned Run Average	Mordecai Brown (1.04, 1906)

1952

Coming off two straight last-place finishes, the Cubs surged to fifth under manager Phil Cavarretta (77-77). Key to the improved performance was a team ERA of 3.58, third best in the league and Hank Sauer's slugging. Sauer tied with the Pirates' Ralph Kiner for the home run title (37 each) and led the league in RBIs (121). Bob Rush and Warren Hacker combined for 29 complete games in 52 starts as Rush was 17-13 and Hacker 15-9. Hacker's ERA of 2.58 was second to New York's Hoyt Wilhelm and was the best for a Cubs pitcher since Hank Borowy's 2.13 for the 1945 pennant-winners. Lefty Paul Minner contributed a 14-9 record with a 3.73. Frank Baumholtz was the best hitter with a .325 average while Toby Atwell led all National League catchers with a .290 average. Defensive problems kept the record from being even better as six men played second base owing to injuries and the team's 123 doubleplays was the lowest total in the league.

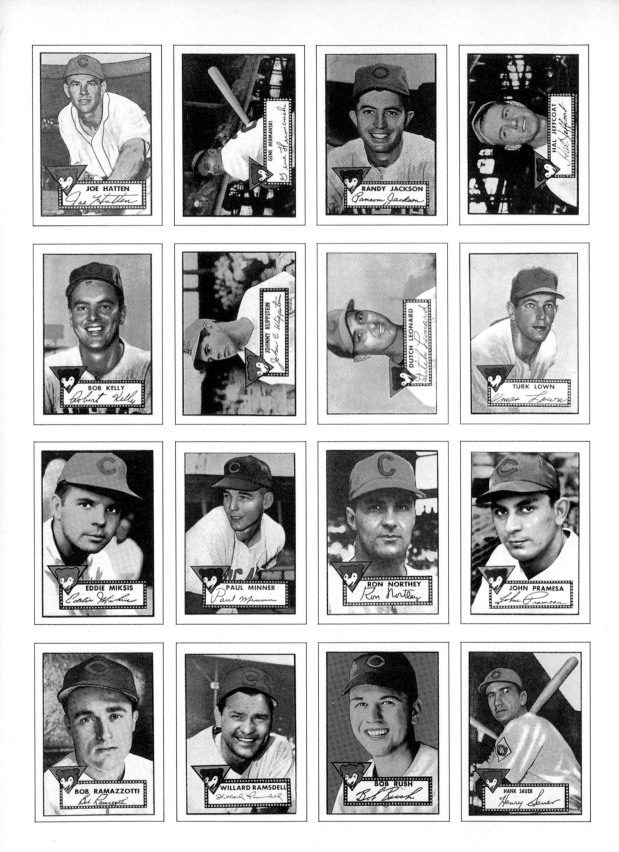

BOB SCHULTZ   BILL SERENA   ROY SMALLEY   BOB USHER

1953

After the excitement of a fifth-place finish the year before, the Cubs staggered home seventh, a full 40 games behind the league leading Brooklyn Dodgers. The difference was only 12 games (77-77 to 65-89). A 14-36 start had the club in the basement for several weeks before a slight upward move into seventh in mid-June. A June trade brought slugging Ralph Kiner from Pittsburgh. Kiner led the team in RBIs (87) despite his late arrival. Overall, Kiner had 35 homers and 116 RBIs, 28 homers coming in the 117 games with the Cubs. Perhaps of even more lasting benefit, however, was the signing, Sept. 8, of two players from the Kansas City Monarchs of the Negro American League—pitcher Bill Dickey and shortstop Ernie Banks. Banks made his Cubs debut on Sept. 17 and hit his first home run on Sept. 20 (off Gerry Staley at St. Louis). Banks was to play 424 straight games before missing one, a record for the start of a career.

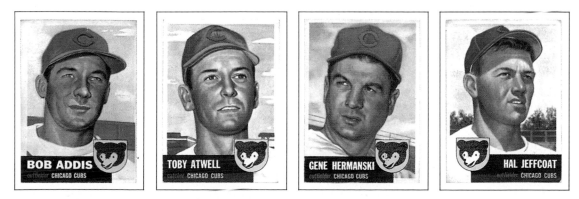

BOB ADDIS
outfielder CHICAGO CUBS

TOBY ATWELL
catcher CHICAGO CUBS

GENE HERMANSKI
outfielder CHICAGO CUBS

HAL JEFFCOAT
outfielder CHICAGO CUBS

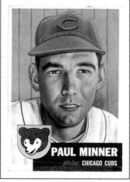

Johnny KLIPPSTEIN
pitcher CHICAGO CUBS

DUTCH LEONARD
pitcher CHICAGO CUBS

TURK LOWN
pitcher CHICAGO CUBS

EDDIE MIKSIS
second base CHICAGO CUBS

PAUL MINNER
pitcher CHICAGO CUBS

HANK SAUER
outfielder CHICAGO CUBS

CARL SAWATSKI
catcher CHICAGO CUBS

BOB SCHULTZ
pitcher CHICAGO CUBS

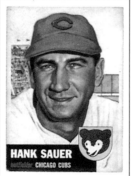
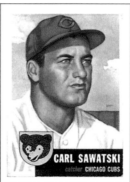
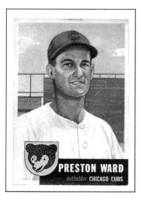

PRESTON WARD
outfielder CHICAGO CUBS

1954

Personnel director Wid Matthews rated the 1954 Cubs as "forty percent stronger" than the previous season's team. Manager Cavarretta, however, did not agree and said so — publicly. As a result, Cavarretta was fired, March 29, an unusual move during spring training, and replaced with Stan Hack. As it turned out, Cavarretta's assessment was more accurate than Matthews' as the Cubs finished seventh again and their record slipped to 64-90, one game worse than 1953. Any chance for improvement in the standings was ruined by a 4-21 June that left the team 21½ games out of first at the end of the month. Hank Sauer was the bright spot, slamming 41 home runs and driving in 103 runs. Ernie Banks began to find a groove and hit 19 homers with 79 RBIs while his doubleplay partner, Gene Baker, had 13 homers and 61 RBIs. A pitching staff showing signs of age contributed to the poor showing. Bob Rush was 13-15, Warren Hacker 6-13 and Paul Minner 11-11.

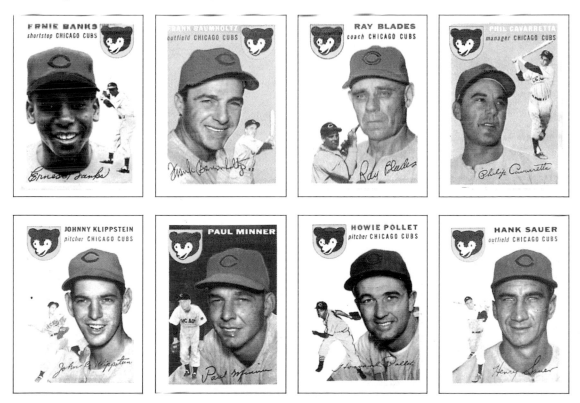

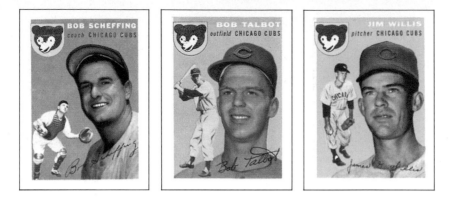

1955

Stan Hack's second season was more interesting and productive than his first, producing a home-run-record achievement by Ernie Banks, the first no-hitter at Wrigley Field since 1917 and an improvement in the standings. At the All-Star break, the Cubs were the surprise of the league with a 45-40 record placing them third. Immediately after the break, however, they lost 12 of 13 games and ultimately finished sixth (72-81), 26 games out. Banks hit .295 with 117 RBIs during the season but also crashed 44 home runs, most ever by a major league shortstop. Banks set the mark on Sept. 2 with his 40th homer, passing the former record of 39 set by Vern Stephens of the Boston Red Sox in 1949. Banks also set a record with five grand slam homers during the season. Sam Jones hurled the no-hitter, defeating the Pirates, 4-0, on May 12 before a crowd of only 2,918.

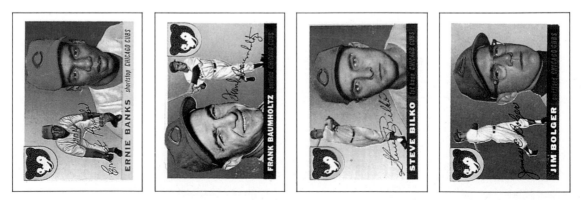

JIM DAVIS pitcher CHICAGO CUBS
STAN HACK manager CHICAGO CUBS
HARRY PERKOWSKI pitcher CHICAGO CUBS
HOWIE POLLET pitcher CHICAGO CUBS
HANK SAUER outfield CHICAGO CUBS
ELVIN TAPPE catcher CHICAGO CUBS
BILL TREMEL pitcher CHICAGO CUBS
GALE WADE outfield CHICAGO CUBS

1956

After some signs of life in 1955, what happened to the Cubs in 1956 had to be in the totally unexpected category. The team got off to a disastrous start and after the first ten days of the season never got higher than sixth in the standings. On Aug. 25, the Cubs fell into the basement and were out of the cellar for only one day thereafter, finishing eighth with a 60-94 record that was the worst in team history. The previous high for defeats in a Cubs season was 93 in 1949. Ernie Banks again had a good year, batting a club-high .297 with 28 home runs. Walt Moryn hit .285 and Dee Fondy .269. Bob Rush had the best season of the pitchers, 13-10, with a 3.19 ERA that was seventh best in the league. Sam Jones was 9-14 ad Warren Hacker only 3-13. Following the season, Stan Hack, who compiled a three-year record of 196-265, was fired as manager and replaced by Bob Scheffing.

1957

New manager Bob Scheffing had very little more success during his first season than his more recent predecessors as the Cubs finished in the second division for the eleventh straight season. The Cubs tied for seventh in the final series of the season, ending up with a 62-92 record, 33 games out of first. On May 1 the Cubs made a trade in an effort to improve the offense, swapping first basemen with the Pirates. In exchange for long-time favorite Dee Fondy, the Cubs got Dale Long as part of the four-player swap. Long hit .298, best on the club, and contributed 21 home runs and 67 RBIs. Ernie Banks, of course, was the big gun with 43 homers, a club-best 102 RBIs and a .285 average. Among the pitchers, 21-year-old rookie righthander Dick Drott was the big winner with a 15-11 record and a 3.58 ERA. Moe Drabowsky was 13-15 and the veteran Bob Rush finished 6-16.

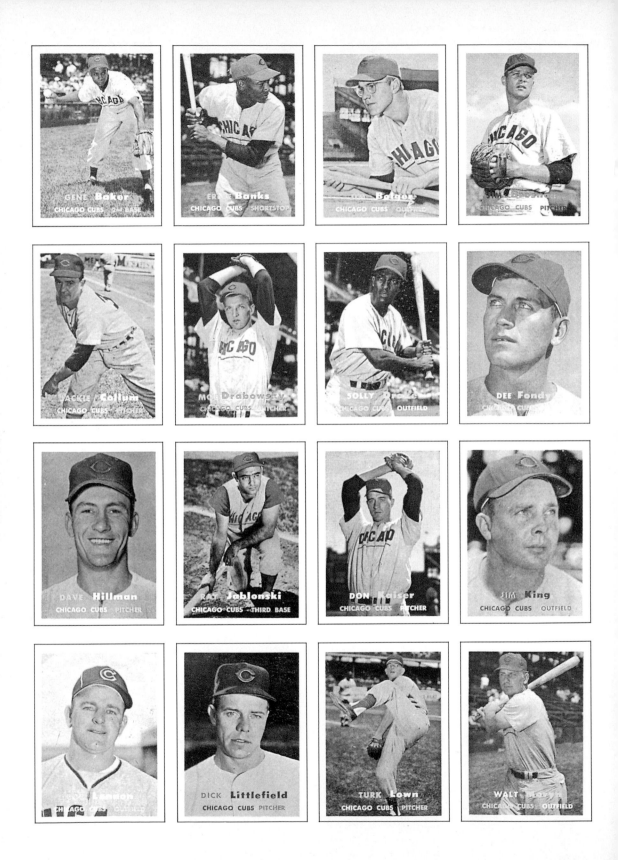

GENE **Baker**
CHICAGO CUBS 2nd BASE

ERNIE **Banks**
CHICAGO CUBS SHORTSTOP

Bolger
CHICAGO CUBS OUTFIELD

CHICAGO CUBS PITCHER

JACKIE **Collum**
CHICAGO CUBS PITCHER

MOE **Drabowsky**
CHICAGO CUBS PITCHER

SOLLY
CHICAGO CUBS OUTFIELD

DEE **Fondy**
CHICAGO CUBS

DAVE **Hillman**
CHICAGO CUBS PITCHER

RAY **Jablonski**
CHICAGO CUBS THIRD BASE

DON **Kaiser**
CHICAGO CUBS PITCHER

JIM **King**
CHICAGO CUBS OUTFIELD

Lennon
CHICAGO CUBS OUTFIELD

DICK **Littlefield**
CHICAGO CUBS PITCHER

TURK **Lown**
CHICAGO CUBS PITCHER

WALT
CHICAGO CUBS OUTFIELD

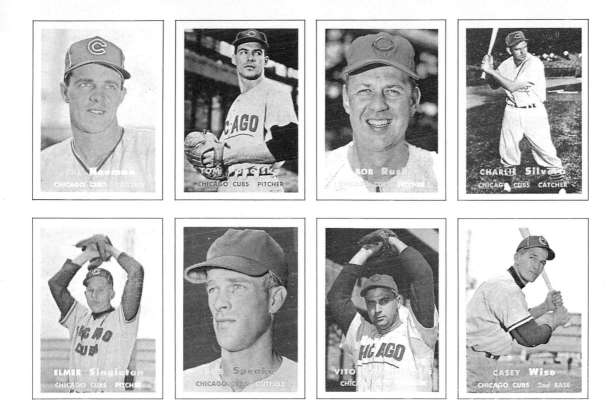

1958

In contrast to the previous season, the Cubs got off to a solid start and stayed in the race well into the season, standing only 2½ games out of first on July 16. Ernie Banks, as usual, was one of the major reasons for the Cubs' performance. Banks was named the Most Valuable Player for his output which included a .313 average and the leadership in both home runs (47) and RBIs (129). Banks had a good deal of help in the longball department as the Cubs led the league with 182 home runs. Dale Long hit .271 with 20 homers and 75 RBIs, veteran outfielder Bobby Thomson added 21 homers and 82 RBIs with a .283 average and outfielder Lee Walls had 24 homers and a .304 average. An elbow injury to righthander Moe Drabowsky hurt the pitching staff in the second half. Drabowsky finished with a 9-11 record after a strong start while Glen Hobbie was 10-6 and Dick Drott, the rookie sensation of 1957, was 7-11. On the final day, the Cubs salvaged a tie for fifth place, the highest finish since 1952.

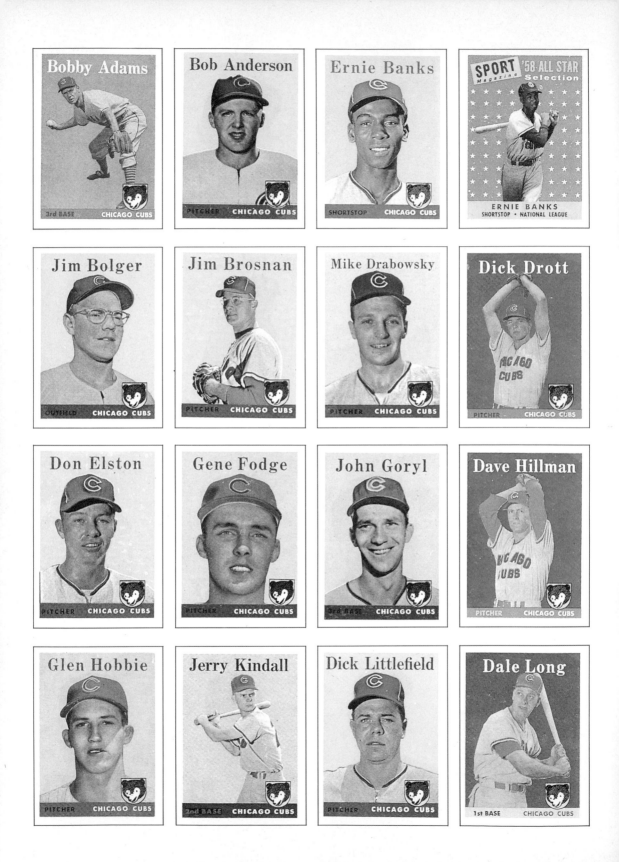

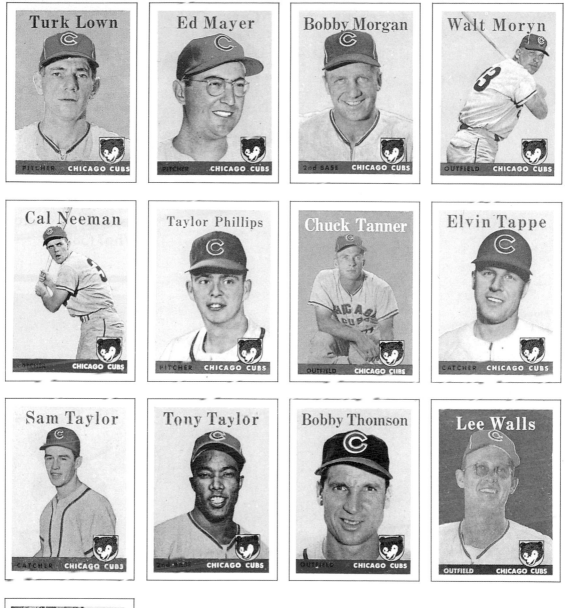

| Turk Lown | Ed Mayer | Bobby Morgan | Walt Moryn |
| PITCHER CHICAGO CUBS | PITCHER CHICAGO CUBS | 2nd BASE CHICAGO CUBS | OUTFIELD CHICAGO CUBS |

| Cal Neeman | Taylor Phillips | Chuck Tanner | Elvin Tappe |
| CATCHER CHICAGO CUBS | PITCHER CHICAGO CUBS | OUTFIELD CHICAGO CUBS | CATCHER CHICAGO CUBS |

| Sam Taylor | Tony Taylor | Bobby Thomson | Lee Walls |
| CATCHER CHICAGO CUBS | 2nd BASE CHICAGO CUBS | OUTFIELD CHICAGO CUBS | OUTFIELD CHICAGO CUBS |

1959

During June the Cubs were as high as third, and as late as July 28 they were only 4½ games out of first place. But, gradually the club sank to another fifth-place tie. Starting on July 28, the Cubs lost seven straight and then suffered a 12-16 August that left them ten games back by the end of the month. One of the most bizarre incidents of the decade in baseball occurred on June 30. Two balls were in play during the fourth inning with Stan Musial of St. Louis running the bases. Musial was called out trying for third and the Cardinals protested that he was tagged with the wrong ball but dropped the protest when they won the game. The Cubs had only one big winner, Glen Hobbie, who was 16-13. Don Elston (10-8) and Bill Henry (9-8) each made 65 appearances out of the bullpen. Ernie Banks had another superb season, batting .304 with major-league leading home run (45) and RBI (143) totals. Despite a 74-80 record, the best in seven seasons, manager Bob Scheffing was fired the day after the season ended.

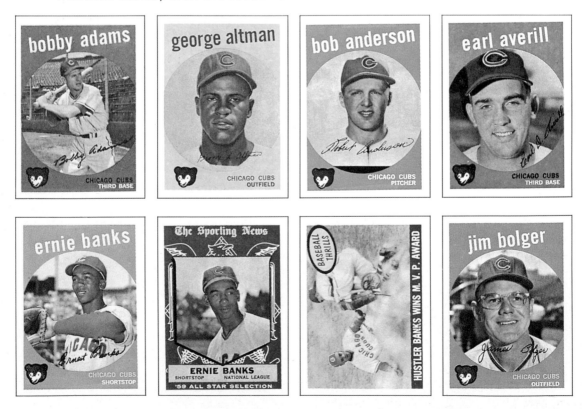

1960

Charlie Grimm started his third term as manager inauspiciously. Under his guidance the team lost 11 of its first 16, and on May 4 Grimm was replaced by Lou Boudreau. The team played no better for Boudreau than it had for Grimm, equalling its standard for losses in a season and finishing seventh (60-94). In 1956, the Cubs also lost 94. Reliever Bill Henry and outfielder Lee Walls were traded to Cincinnati for slugging third baseman Frank Thomas. Thomas hit 21 homers while batting only .238 with 64 RBIs in 135 games. Former Phillies outfielder Richie Ashburn led the club with a .291 average but Ernie Banks was again the big gun, turning in his fourth straight 40-homer season. Banks hit .271 with 41 home runs and 117 RBIs. On Sept. 13 Danny Murphy, just 20 days past his 18th birthday, became the youngest Cubs player ever to hit a home run when he smacked one at Cincinnati. Glen Hobbie (16-20) was again the leading pitcher.

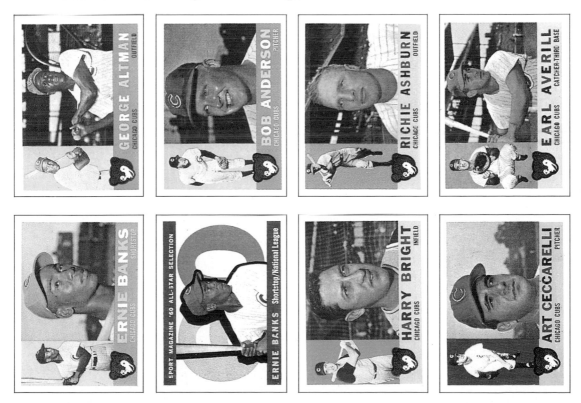

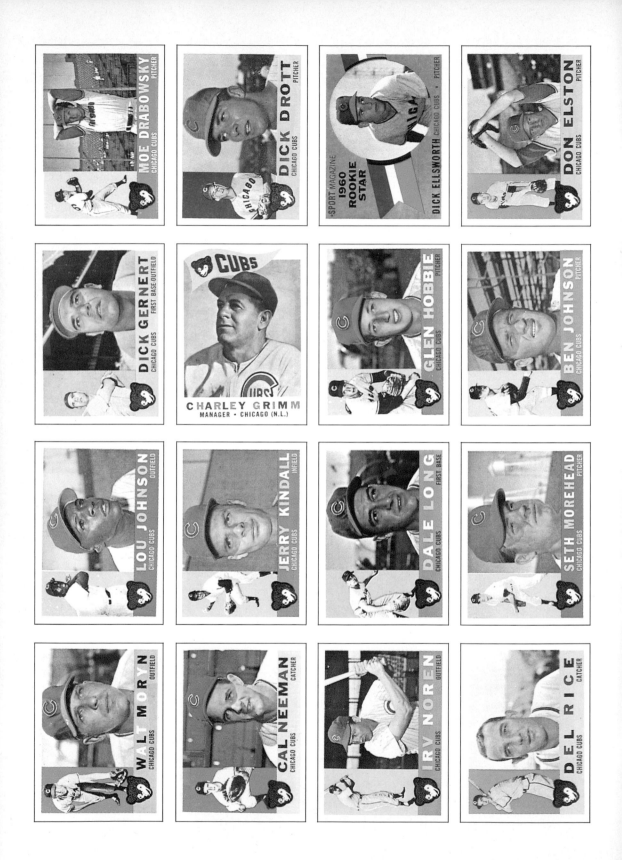

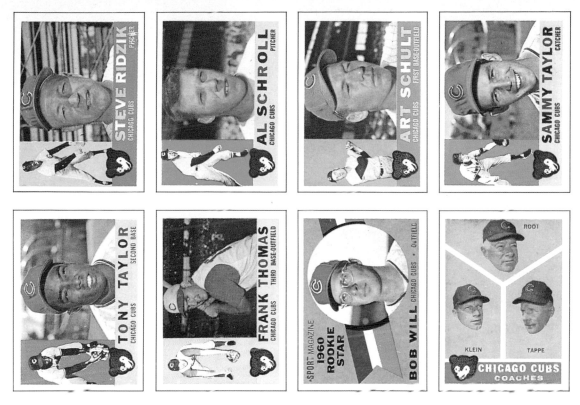

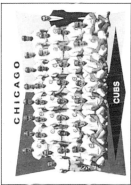

1961

Lou Boudreau became the only manager in baseball history to be dismissed to make way for eight successors. Owner Philip K. Wrigley determined to replace him with a "college of coaches." Eight coaches were named for the 1961 season and half of them—Harry Craft, Vedie Himsl, Lou Klein and Elvin Tappe—acted as head coach on a rotating basis during some part of the season.

Following an 8-8 start in April, the Cubs collapsed despite their unique system of leadership and were out of the race by the end of May, losing 18 of 25 games during that month. A knee injury to Ernie Banks ended his 717-game consecutive streak on June 23. Later, Banks was troubled by a lack of depth perception in his left eye and finished with a .277 average, 29 home runs and 80 RBIs in 138 games. George Altman led in batting (.303) and RBIs (96) while hitting 27 homers. Don Cardwell led the pitchers with a 15-14 record. At season's end the Cubs were seventh with a 64-90 record, 29 games out of first.

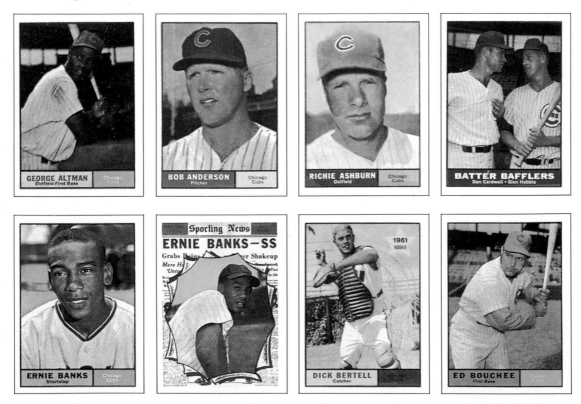

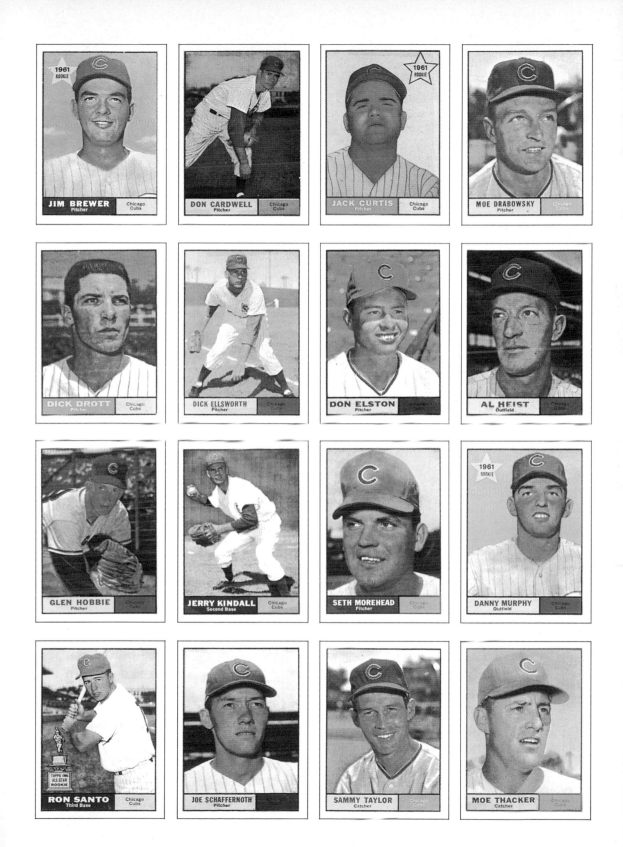

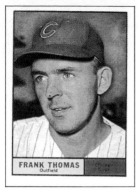

FRANK THOMAS
Outfield

BOB WILL
Outfield

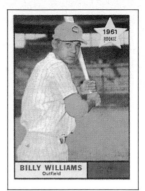

BILLY WILLIAMS
Outfield

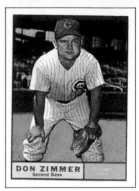

DON ZIMMER
Second Base

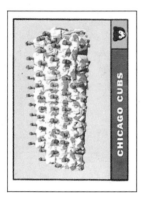

CHICAGO CUBS

1962

In the second season of the college of coaches some spectacular statistics were accumulated, virtually all negative. With a final record of 59-103, the team became the first 100-loss club in Cubs history, matching the major league record for second-division finishes (16 straight years) with a ninth-place finish in the expanded National League. Only the dreadful New York Mets (40-120) allowed the Cubs to escape an even worse fate. As it was, they finished behind one first-year team (the Houston Colt .45s) and drew only 609,802 to Wrigley Field, the lowest total in the major leagues and worst for the Cubs since 1943. George Altman (.318) was the only regular to hit .300 but Ernie Banks returned to something of his former form with a .269 average, 37 home runs and 104 RBIs in 154 games. Smooth-fielding Ken Hubbs was established at second base and hit .260. Lou Brock hit .263 and stole 16 bases.

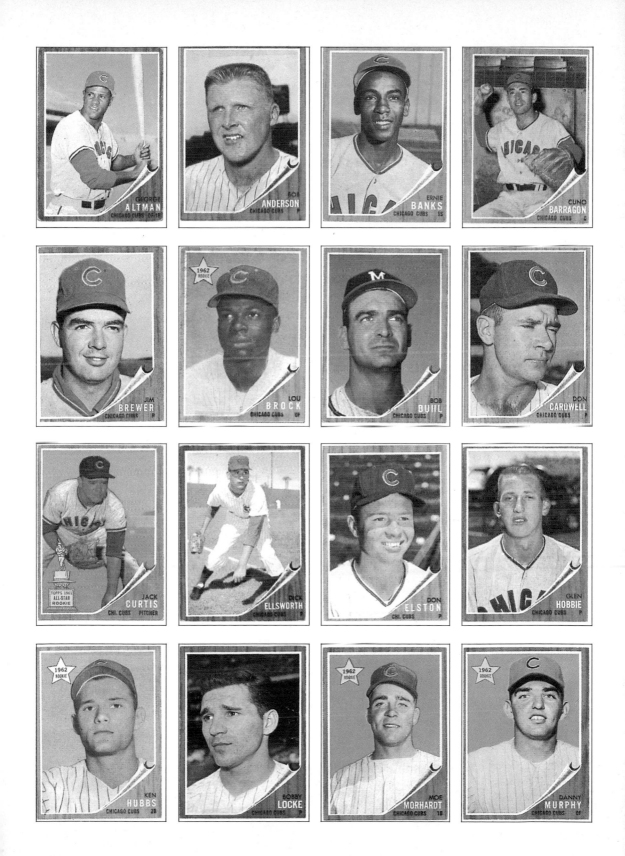

≡1963≡

The college of coaches concept had begun to wobble in 1962, and in 1963 owner Wrigley decided to have one head coach, Bob Kennedy. He also decided to add an athletic director, another first for baseball. The athletic director was retired Air Force Col. Robert V. Whitlow, who moved in on Feb. 1, 1963, and lasted until he resigned on Jan 7, 1965.

Under Kennedy the Cubs were 82-80, putting them over .500 for the first time since 1946. However, the team finished seventh in the ten-team league, extending its second-division record to a major league-record 17 straight years, 17 games out at season's end. Ron Santo (.297) and Billy Williams (.286) hit 25 home runs each with Santo leading the team with 99 RBIs to Williams' 95. Dick Ellsworth had an outstanding 22-10 record and 2.11 ERA and Lindy McDaniel was 13-7 out of the bullpen.

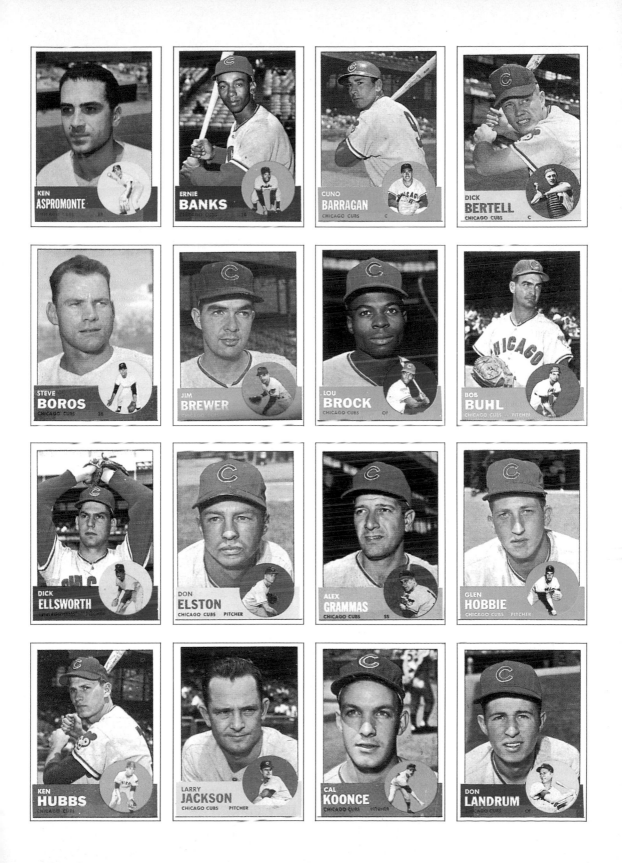

KEN
ASPROMONTE
CHICAGO CUBS 2B

ERNIE
BANKS
CHICAGO CUBS 1B

CUNO
BARRAGAN
CHICAGO CUBS C

DICK
BERTELL
CHICAGO CUBS C

STEVE
BOROS
CHICAGO CUBS 3B

JIM
BREWER
CHICAGO CUBS

LOU
BROCK
CHICAGO CUBS OF

BOB
BUHL
CHICAGO CUBS PITCHER

DICK
ELLSWORTH
CHICAGO CUBS PITCHER

DON
ELSTON
CHICAGO CUBS PITCHER

ALEX
GRAMMAS
CHICAGO CUBS SS

GLEN
HOBBIE
CHICAGO CUBS PITCHER

KEN
HUBBS
CHICAGO CUBS

LARRY
JACKSON
CHICAGO CUBS PITCHER

CAL
KOONCE
CHICAGO CUBS PITCHER

DON
LANDRUM
CHICAGO CUBS OF

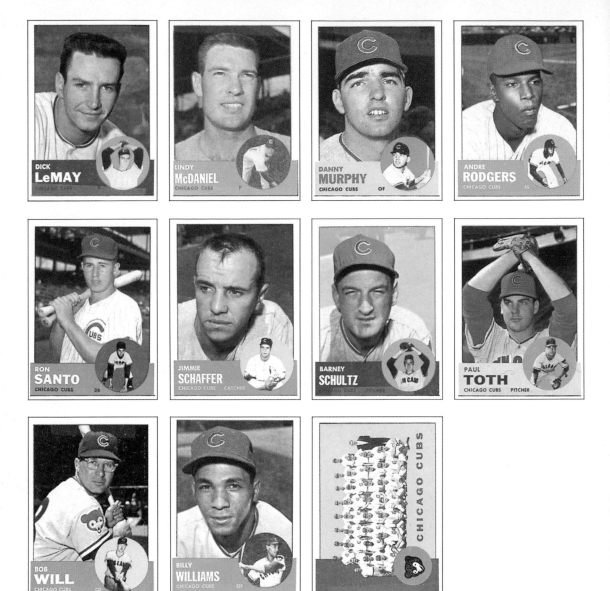

1964

This was a season that was a tragedy before it even began. On Feb. 15, 1964, Ken Hubbs was killed in a private-plane crash near Provo, Utah. One of the premier second basemen during the previous two seasons, in his rookie year Hubbs had flawlessly handled 418 chances over 78 consecutive games.

While the college of coaches was technically still in effect, Bob Kennedy, who had "coached" the entire season in 1963, did the same in 1964 although the Cubs were 76-86 and finished eighth in the 10-team league. Ron Santo and Billy Williams continued to develop into top hitters. Santo batted .313, hit 30 homers and was second in the league with 114 RBIs. Williams led the club with 33 homers, hitting .312 with 98 RBIs. Ernie Banks, now firmly settled at first base, hit for a .264 average with 23 homers and 95 RBIs. Larry Jackson was the star pitcher with a 24-11 record, the most victories for a Cubs pitcher since Charlie Root was 26-15 in 1927.

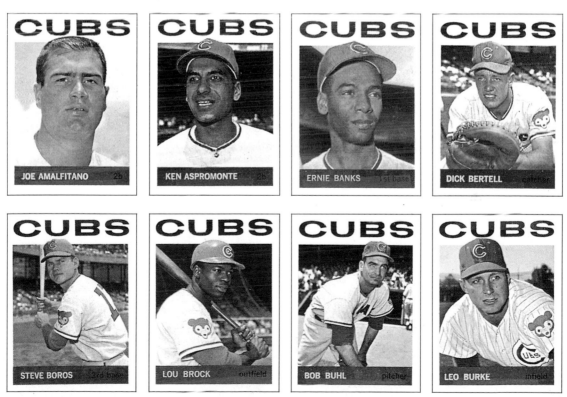

JOE AMALFITANO 2b

KEN ASPROMONTE 2b

ERNIE BANKS 1st base

DICK BERTELL catcher

STEVE BOROS 3rd base

LOU BROCK outfield

BOB BUHL pitcher

LEO BURKE infield

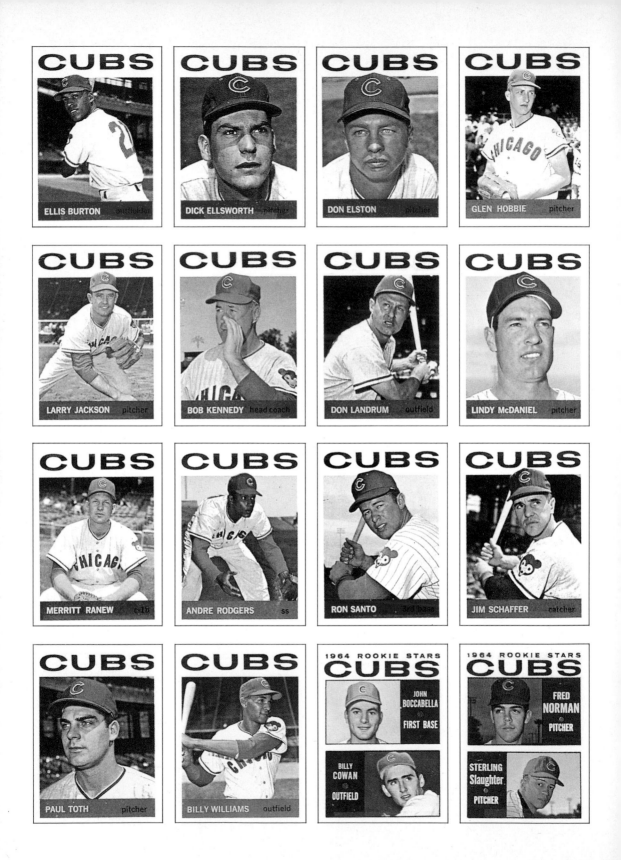

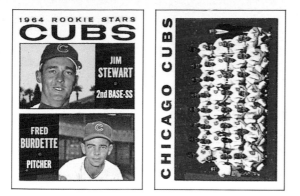

1965

This, as it turned out, was the final season for the college of coaches concept that so fascinated owner Philip K. Wrigley. Bob Kennedy, who had "coached" all of the Cubs games for each of the two prior seasons, handled the team for 56 games (24-32). Lou Klein returned as "head coach" for the other 106 games (48-58), leaving the club 72-90 overall and eighth. (Kennedy later became the general manager.) Billy Williams, in one of his finest all-around seasons, finished among the top four in the league in almost all offensive categories. He was fourth in batting (.315), second in doubles (39), third in homers (34) and fourth in RBIs (108). Banks had another strong season, hitting .265 with 28 homers and 106 RBIs; Ron Santo (.285) hit 33 homers and had 101 RBIs, giving the Cubs three 100-RBI men in the same season for the first time since 1930. Larry Jackson slumped to 14-21 but still tied for the leadership in wins with Dick Ellsworth (14-15).

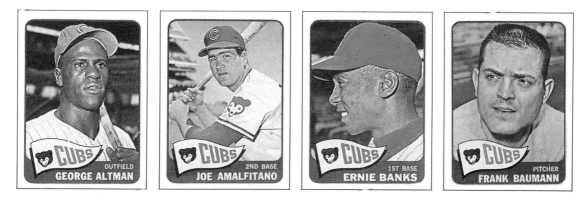

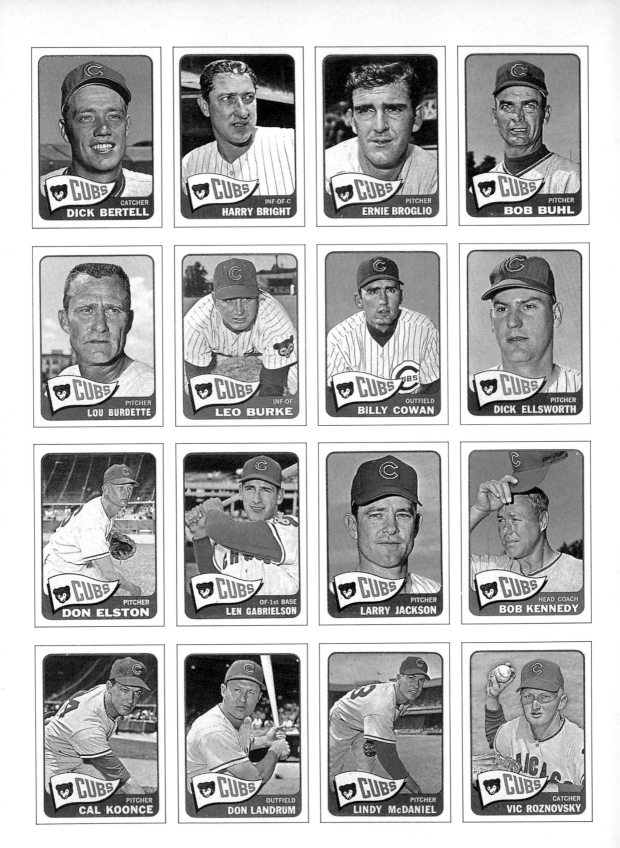

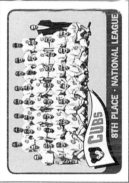

1966

Wind is always a factor at Wrigley Field but the winds of changes blew with a seldom-seen fierceness in 1966. First, Leo Durocher was named manager, ending the college of coaches. Then, trades sent away Ted Abernathy (whose 31 saves led the league in 1965), his bullpen partner Lindy McDaniel and starters Larry Jackson and Bob Buhl. Buhl, whose acquisition was one of the top trades in Cubs history, went away in an even better deal, going to the Phillies for pitcher Ferguson Jenkins, outfielder Adolpho Phillips and first baseman John Herrnstein on April 21, along with Jackson. McDaniel went to San Francisco on Dec. 2, 1965, for catcher Randy Hundley and pitcher Bill Hands and Abernathy went to Atlanta for outfielder Lee Thomas and a minor league pitcher, lefthander Arnold Early. Durocher's first season resulted in the lowest finish in Cubs history, tenth, with a 59-103 record, marking the second time in five seasons the team lost a record 103 games.

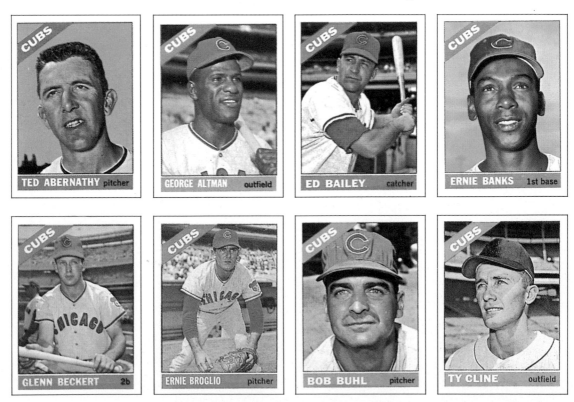

TED ABERNATHY pitcher

GEORGE ALTMAN outfield

ED BAILEY catcher

ERNIE BANKS 1st base

GLENN BECKERT 2b

ERNIE BROGLIO pitcher

BOB BUHL pitcher

TY CLINE outfield

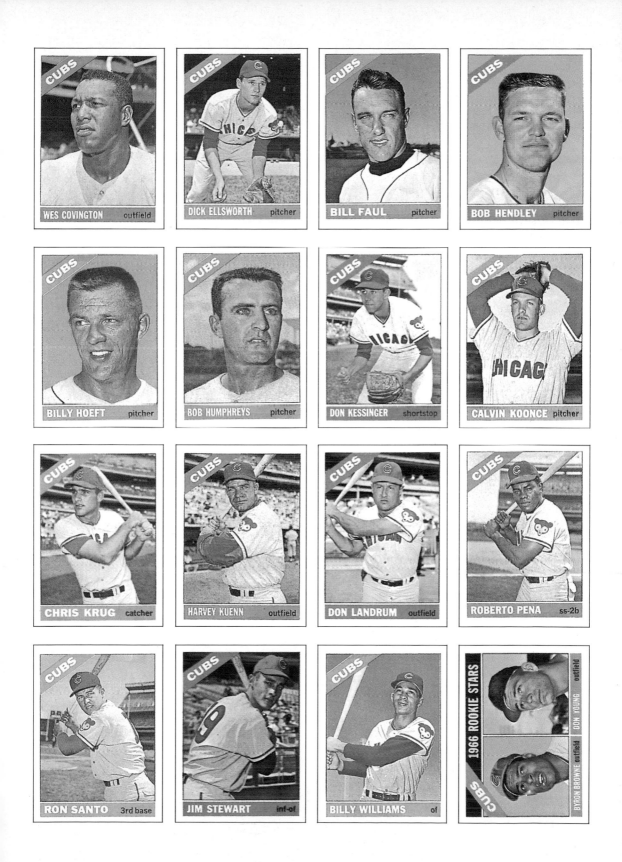

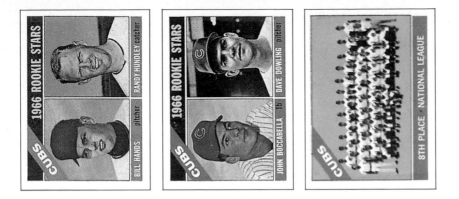

1967

Having undergone a housecleaning of major proportions in 1966, the Cubs showed a dramatic turnaround in 1967, zooming to third place in the National League with a 87-74 record, an improvement of 28 games in a single season as well as seven spots in the standings. Ferguson Jenkins produced the first of his sixth straight 20-win seasons with a 20-13 record, a 2.80 ERA and 20 complete games, the best in the league. Ron Santo reached the 30-homer plateau for the fourth straight season, hitting a club-high 31 while batting .300 with 98 RBIs (also tops on the Cubs). Billy Williams (.278) had 28 homers and 84 RBIs and Ernie Banks (.276) had 23 homers and drove in 95. The Cubs were not only third but missed second by only 2 ½ games as San Francisco finished at 91-71. Attendance improved by more than fifty percent to 977,226.

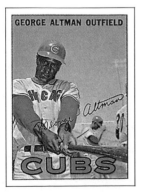

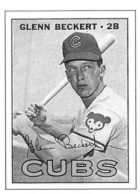

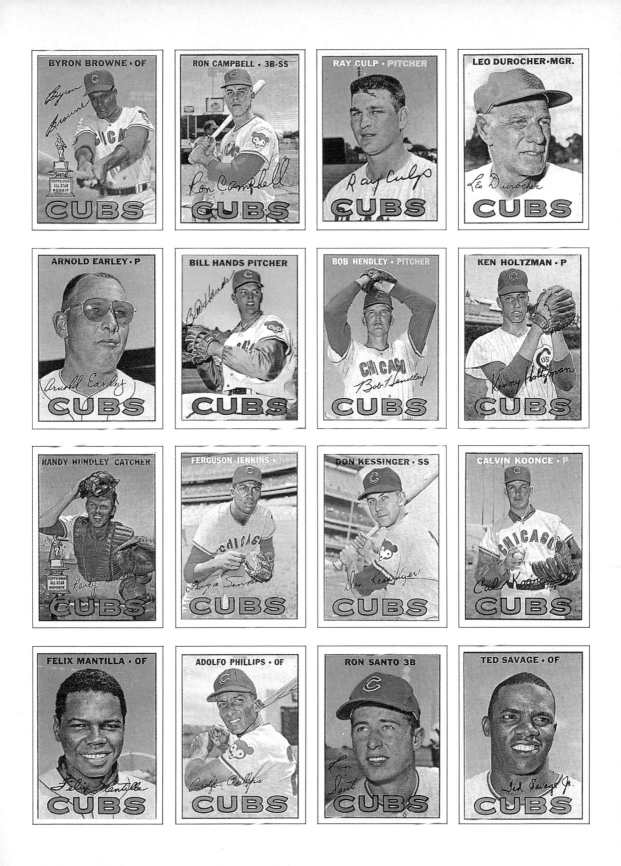

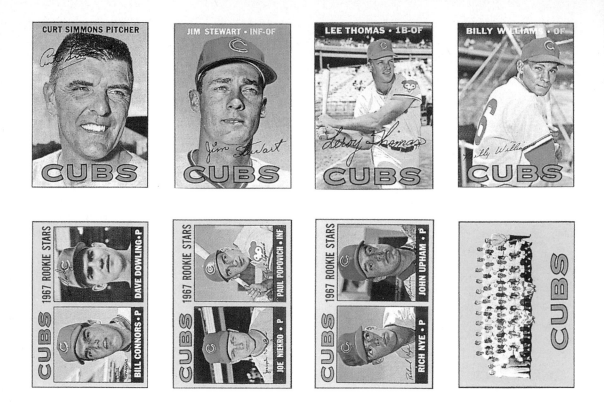

CURT SIMMONS PITCHER — CUBS

JIM STEWART · INF-OF — CUBS

LEE THOMAS · 1B-OF — CUBS

BILLY WILLIAMS · OF — CUBS

1967 ROOKIE STARS — DAVE DOWLING · P / BILL CONNORS · P — CUBS

1967 ROOKIE STARS — PAUL POPOVICH · INF / JOE NIEKRO · P — CUBS

1967 ROOKIE STARS — JOHN UPHAM · P / RICH NYE · P — CUBS

CUBS

1968

Although Glenn Beckert had a 27-game hitting streak, the first 100 games were more of a struggle than either manager Leo Durocher or most baseball observers expected. Finally, the club went over .500 by sweeping a doubleheader on July 28 at Wrigley. An 8-3 win behind Joe Niekro in the opener and a 1-0 shutout by Ken Holtzman in the nightcap gave the Cubs a 52-51 record. The doubleheader drew a crowd of 42,261, largest for the Cubs at home since 1948. A 32-27 mark over the final two months enabled the team to finish (84-78) third for the second straight year. Ernie Banks, who hit .246, was third in the league with 32 homers and batted in 83 runs. Beckert, who had 189 hits (third in the league) batted .294 and Ron Santo and Billy Williams were again the power twins. Santo (.246) had 26 homers and Williams (.288) had 30. Each drove in 98 runs, second best totals in the league. Ferguson Jenkins was 20-15 with a 2.63 ERA, Bill Hands was 16-10, Holtzman 11-14 and Niekro 14-10.

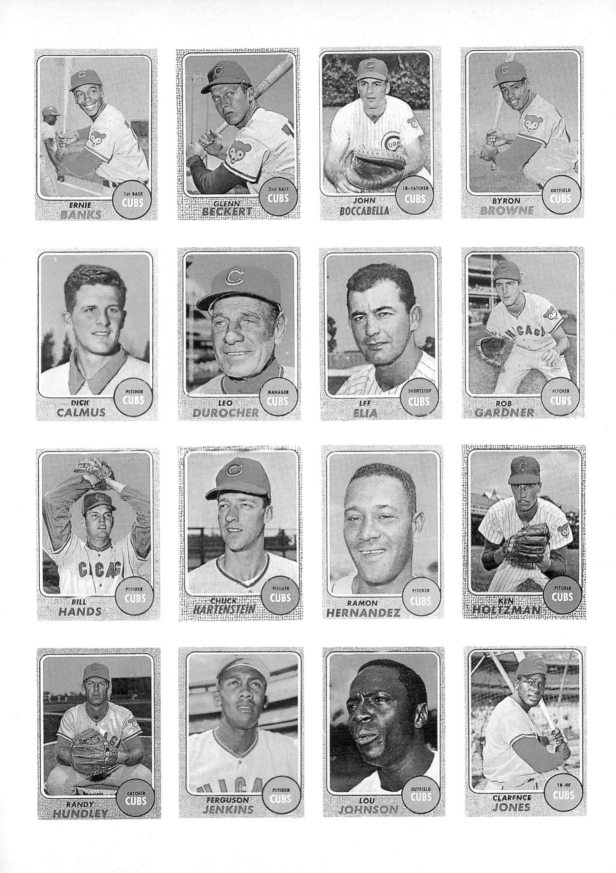

ERNIE **BANKS** — 1st BASE — CUBS

GLENN **BECKERT** — 2nd BASE — CUBS

JOHN **BOCCABELLA** — 1B-CATCHER — CUBS

BYRON **BROWNE** — OUTFIELD — CUBS

DICK **CALMUS** — PITCHER — CUBS

LEO **DUROCHER** — MANAGER — CUBS

LEE **ELIA** — SHORTSTOP — CUBS

ROB **GARDNER** — PITCHER — CUBS

BILL **HANDS** — PITCHER — CUBS

CHUCK **HARTENSTEIN** — PITCHER — CUBS

RAMON **HERNANDEZ** — PITCHER — CUBS

KEN **HOLTZMAN** — PITCHER — CUBS

RANDY **HUNDLEY** — CATCHER — CUBS

FERGUSON **JENKINS** — PITCHER — CUBS

LOU **JOHNSON** — OUTFIELD — CUBS

CLARENCE **JONES** — 1B-OF — CUBS

DON
KESSINGER
SHORTSTOP
CUBS

PETE
MIKKELSEN
PITCHER
CUBS

DICK
NEN
1st BASE
CUBS

JOE
NIEKRO
PITCHER
CUBS

RICH
NYE
PITCHER
CUBS

ADOLFO
PHILLIPS
OUTFIELD
CUBS

RON
SANTO
3rd BASE
CUBS

RON SANTO
THIRD BASE
NATIONAL LEAGUE
The Sporting News
ALL-STAR SELECTION

TED
SAVAGE
OUTFIELD
CUBS

AL
SPANGLER
OUTFIELD
CUBS

JOHN
STEPHENSON
CATCHER
CUBS

BILL
STONEMAN
PITCHER
CUBS

BILLY
WILLIAMS
OUTFIELD
CUBS

1968 ROOKIE STARS
BILL SCHLESINGER · OF
JOSE ARCIA · SS
CUBS

1969

Rolling up their best record since 1945, and leading the league for 155 straight days, the Cubs did everything that could be expected of them in 1969 with one exception—win the pennant. After commanding the National League East for the entire season, the Cubs hit a tailspin in September while the New York Mets won 38 of their last 49 and it was New York, not Chicago, on top at season's end. On Aug. 14 the Cubs had an 8½-game lead over second-place St. Louis and 9½ over third-place New York. By Sept. 2 it was still five games over the now-second Mets. Then came September when the Cubs were 9-17.

For the first time since 1935, the team had two 20-game winners, Ferguson Jenkins (21-15) and Bill Hands (20-14). Ron Santo enjoyed a banner season, hitting .289 with 29 homers and 123 RBIs while 38-year-old Ernie Banks had a heroic year, batting .253 with 23 homers and 106 RBIs. Billy Williams hit .293 with 23 homers and 95 RBIs.

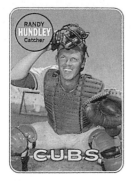

RANDY HUNDLEY
Catcher
CUBS

FERGIE JENKINS
Pitcher
CHICAGO
CUBS

DON KESSINGER
Shortstop
CUBS

The Sporting News
DON KESSINGER
Shortstop
CUBS
NATIONAL LEAGUE ALL-STARS

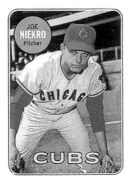

JOE NIEKRO
Pitcher
CHICAG
CUBS

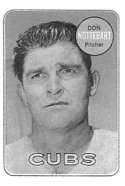

DON NOTTEBART
Pitcher
CUBS

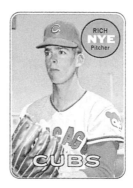

RICH NYE
Pitcher
CHICAG
CUBS

GENE OLIVER
Catcher
CUBS

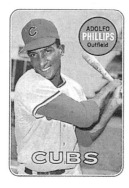

ADOLFO PHILLIPS
Outfield
CUBS

PHIL REGAN
Pitcher
CUBS

The Sporting News
RON SANTO
3rd Base
CUBS
NATIONAL LEAGUE ALL-STARS

RON SANTO
3rd Base
CUBS

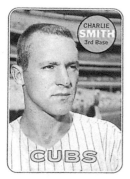

CHARLIE SMITH
3rd Base
CUBS

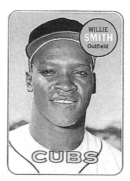

WILLIE SMITH
Outfield
CUBS

AL SPANGLER
Outfield
CUBS

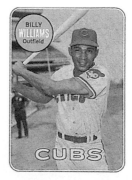

BILLY WILLIAMS
Outfield
CHICAGO
CUBS

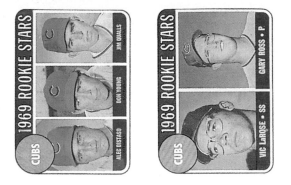

1970

Attempting to recover from the fatal collapse of 1969, the Cubs started strong in 1970, responding to the urging of manager Durocher. But, ultimately, the result was the same, only the fade started sooner and the Cubs fans were spared the agony of September. From April 22 to June 24, a period of 64 straight days, the team was first in the National League East. However, from that point on, the race belonged mostly to the Pirates. Although the Cubs challenged during most of the summer, the Pirates finished five games in front of the Cubs' 84-78 record. Billy Williams had perhaps his finest all-around season, batting .322 with 42 home runs and 129 RBIs, but still lost the spotlight to "Mr. Cub," Ernie Banks. Banks connected for the 500th home run of his illustrious career on May 12, hitting a second-inning shot off Atlanta's Pat Jarvis that also accounted for his 1600th career RBI.

Ted Abernathy | PITCHER

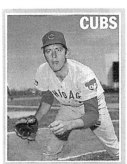

Hank Aguirre | PITCHER

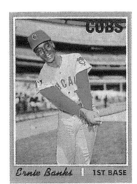

Ernie Banks | 1ST BASE

Glenn Beckert | 2ND BASE

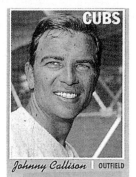
Johnny Callison | OUTFIELD

Leo Durocher | MANAGER

Jimmie Hall | OUTFIELD

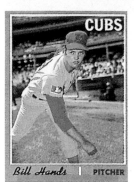
Bill Hands | PITCHER

Bill Heath | CATCHER

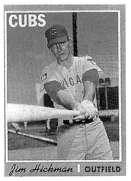
Jim Hickman | OUTFIELD

Ken Holtzman | PITCHER

Randy Hundley | CATCHER

Fergie Jenkins | PITCHER

Don Kessinger | SHORTSTOP

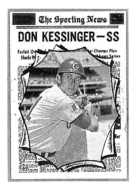
The Sporting News
DON KESSINGER—SS

Nate Oliver | INFIELD

Paul Popovich | 2ND BASE

Jim Qualls | OUTFIELD

Phil Regan | PITCHER

Ken Rudolph | CATCHER

≡1971

Despite losing 11 of their first 16, the Cubs managed to bootstrap themselves back into the race in the National League East, surging to within 4½ games of first place by late August. On Aug. 20 the Cubs swept a doubleheader from Houston to cap a drive that began with an 18-9 record in June. But then came 18 losses in the next 24 games, including five to first-place Pittsburgh in the first two weeks of September and the Cubs settled for a third-place tie with an 83-79 record, 14 games behind the Pirates. Ferguson Jenkins was one of the primary reasons for the drive. Jenkins, the Cy Young winner in the N.L., was 24-13 with a 2.77 ERA and a staggering 30 complete games in 39 starts. Second baseman Glenn Beckert hit .342 while Billy Williams (.301) led the club with 30 homers, 86 runs scored and 93 RBIs. Ken Holtzman shared the spotlight by pitching his second no-hitter in three years. His first was against Atlanta on Aug. 19, 1969 and his second came June 3, 1971, a 1-0 victory over Cincinnati.

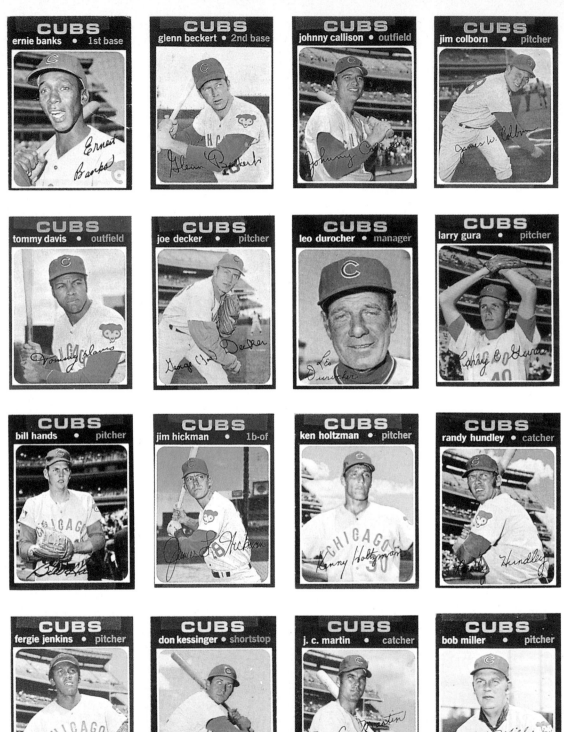

CUBS
milt pappas • pitcher

CUBS
joe pepitone • of-1b

CUBS
juan pizarro • pitcher

CUBS
paul popovich • infield

CUBS
phil regan • pitcher

CUBS
roberto rodriquez • p

CUBS
ken rudolph • catcher

CUBS
ron santo • 3rd base

CUBS
hector torres • 2b-ss

CUBS
hoyt wilhelm • pitcher

CUBS
billy williams • outfield

1971 ROOKIE STARS
CUBS
jim dunegan • pitcher

roe skidmore • first base

1971 ROOKIE STARS CUBS

GARRY JESTADT

BROCK DAVIS

ADRIAN GARRETT

CUBS

1972

This was a season in which Billy Williams became the first Cubs player to win a batting championship since 1945, two Cubs pitched no-hitters (one of them a nearly perfect game) and Ferguson Jenkins logged his sixth straight 20-win season, but the Cubs finished second for the third time in four seasons with an 85-70 record. Williams batted .333 to become the first Cubs batting king since Phil Cavarretta. Williams also clouted 37 homers in a season delayed 15 days by the players' strike. Burt Hooton pitched the first no-hitter, on only the second day of play. It was Hooton's fourth big-league start and it came on April 16, a 4-0 victory over the Phillies at Wrigley Field. Milt Pappas hurled the near-perfect effort on Sept. 2, winning 8-0 over San Diego. Pappas walked Larry Stahl on a 3-2 pitch with two out in the ninth. On July 24, manager Leo Durocher resigned and was replaced by coach, Whitey Lockman. Durocher's 452 wins were the fourth best ever by a Cubs manager.

GLENN BECKERT

GLENN BECKERT IN ACTION

BILL BONHAM

HAL BREEDEN

JOHNNY CALLISON

JOSE CARDENAL

JOE DECKER

LEO DUROCHER

STEVE HAMILTON

BILL HANDS

JIM HICKMAN

RANDY HUNDLEY

CLEO JAMES

FERGIE JENKINS

DON KESSINGER

J. C. MARTIN

RICK MONDAY

RAY NEWMAN

MILT PAPPAS

JOE PEPITONE

JOE PEPITONE
IN ACTION

JUAN PIZARRO

PAUL POPOVICH

PHIL REGAN

1973

One of the more inexplicable seasons in Cubs history, 1973 presented an opportunity for a divisional title that evaporated for a reason or reasons unknown. In May they started a seven-game winning streak that paved the way for 13 wins in 17 games and helped produce a record of 30-19, moving them into first place. On June 29, Jose Cardenal's 10th-inning hit off reliever Buzz Capra gave the Cubs a 4-3 win over the Mets and left them eight games ahead of the pack. Even though no major injuries intervened, the Cubs skidded through a 9-19 July and were knocked out of first place for good on July 22 when the Giants won a 13-inning game, 4-1, to complete a three-game sweep. Finally, a 77-84 record left the Cubs five games behind first-place New York. Three pitchers won 14 games each though all had losing records: Ferguson Jenkins (14-16), Rick Reuschel (14-15) and Burt Hooton (14-17). Cardenal (.303) was the only regular over .300 while Billy Williams dropped to .288.

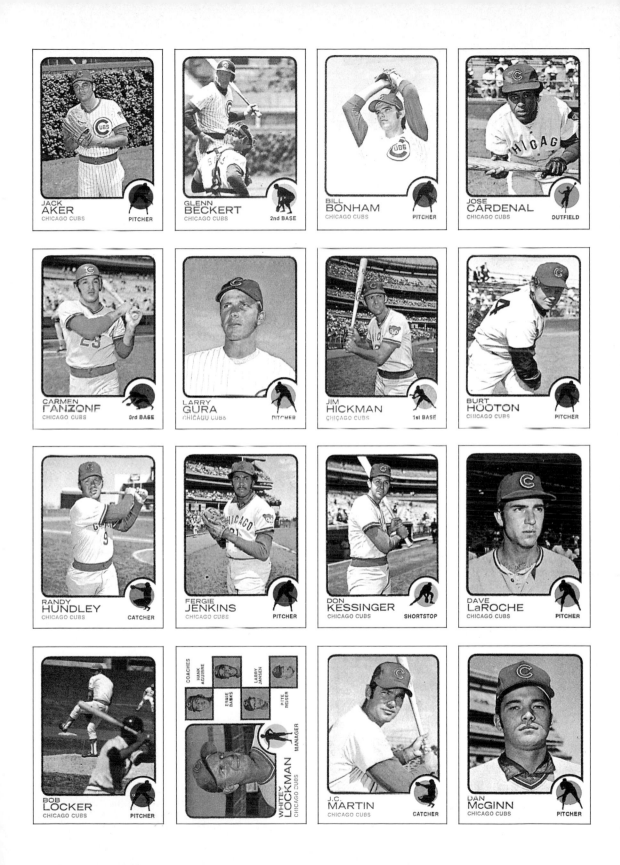

RICK
MONDAY
CHICAGO CUBS
OUTFIELD

MILT
PAPPAS
CHICAGO CUBS
PITCHER

JOE
PEPITONE
CHICAGO CUBS
1st BASE

PAUL
POPOVICH
CHICAGO CUBS
2nd BASE

RICK
REUSCHEL
CHICAGO CUBS
PITCHER

KEN
RUDOLPH
CHICAGO CUBS
CATCHER

RON
SANTO
CHICAGO CUBS
3rd BASE

BILLY
WILLIAMS
CHICAGO CUBS
OUTFIELD

CHICAGO CUBS

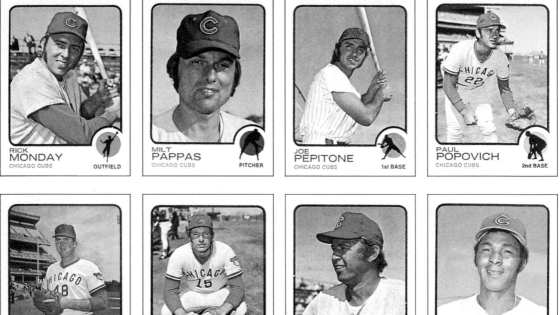

1974

Only five games out at the end of 1973, the Cubs had finished fifth, and committed to a youth movement for the following season. In 1974 the Cubs were so inexperienced that the pitcher with most career wins was Burt Hooton who had only 27 victories to his credit. After the season, Billy Williams was traded to Oakland in an Oct. 23 deal that brought two pitchers and infielder Manny Trillo to the Cubs. In 15 full seasons, Williams batted .296 with 392 homers for the Cubs. Rick Monday led the hitters with a .293 average and 20 home runs though only 58 RBIs. Jose Cardenal hit .293 and Jerry Morales, obtained from San Diego, hit .273 with a club-high 82 RBIs. Second-year man Rick Reuschel was 13-12 as the top pitcher while Bill Bonham was 11-22. Lockman resigned at mid-season and was replaced by Jim Marshall as the club skidded into the cellar with a 66-96 mark.

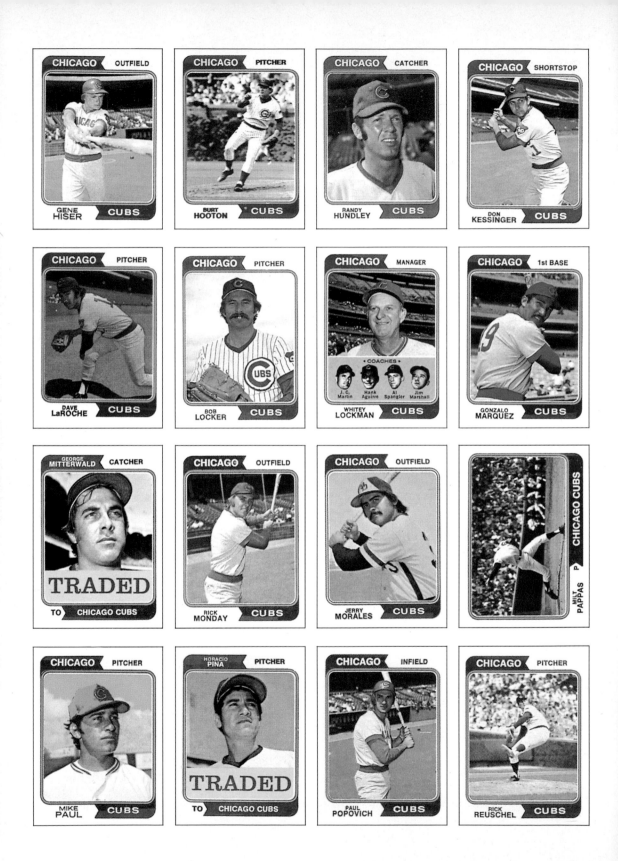

1975

Jim Marshall's first full season as Cubs manager was something of a modest success in that the club moved from last in the National League East to a tie for fifth with a 75-87 record. But what grabbed attention was Bill Madlock's rise to batting champion with a .354 average. It was the second time in four years a Cub had led the league in hitting after a period of 28 years without such an accomplishment. As it was, Madlock was only the fourth Cubs player since 1888 to lead the N.L. batters. Jose Cardenal hit .317 and finished ninth in the league while Andre Thornton batted .293. But the club hit only 95 home runs. On Aug. 21 Rick Reuschel and Paul Reuschel combined for a 7-0 shutout of Los Angeles, the first time brothers had ever shared a major league shutout. Rick Reuschel finished at 11-17 with a 3.73 ERA while Paul, a mid-season callup from the minors, was 1-3.

CUBS

BILL BONHAM — Pitcher

CUBS

RAY BURRIS — Pitcher

CUBS

JOSE CARDENAL — Outfield

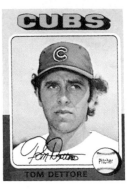

CUBS

TOM DETTORE — Pitcher

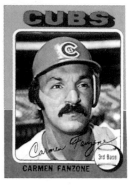

CUBS

CARMEN FANZONE — 3rd Base

CUBS

KEN FRAILING — Pitcher

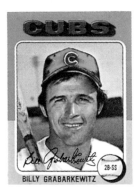

CUBS

BILLY GRABARKEWITZ — 2B-SS

CUBS

VIC HARRIS — 2nd Base

CUBS

BURT HOOTON — Pitcher

CUBS

DON KESSINGER — Shortstop

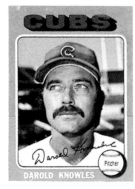

CUBS

DAROLD KNOWLES — Pitcher

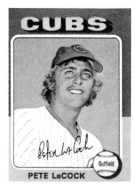

CUBS

PETE LaCOCK — Outfield

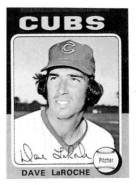

CUBS

DAVE LaROCHE — Pitcher

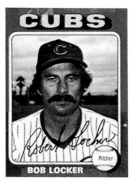

CUBS

BOB LOCKER — Pitcher

CUBS

BILL MADLOCK — 3rd Base

CUBS

GEORGE MITTERWALD — Catcher

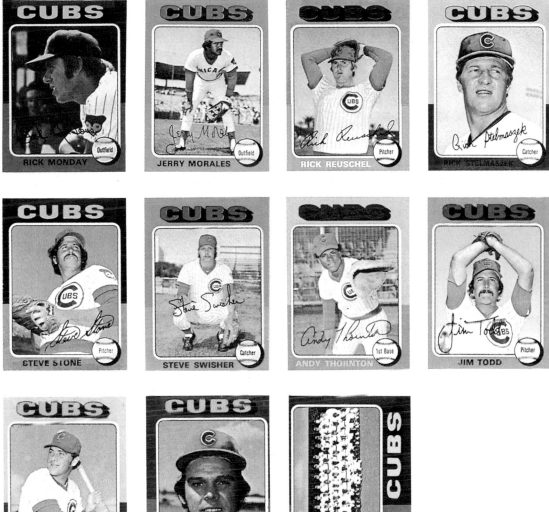

RICK MONDAY — Outfield

JERRY MORALES — Outfield

RICK REUSCHEL — Pitcher

RICK STELMASZEK — Catcher

STEVE STONE — Pitcher

STEVE SWISHER — Catcher

ANDY THORNTON — 1st Base

JIM TODD — Pitcher

CHRIS WARD — Outfield

OSCAR ZAMORA — Pitcher

CUBS

1976

All success, it has been said, is relative, and certainly that was the case for the 1976 Cubs. The team finished with the same record (75-87) as the season before, but instead of tying for fifth the Cubs finished fourth, 26 games behind. What made a record of that proportion even possible was strong finishes by two players—pitcher Ray Burris and third baseman Bill Madlock. Madlock emerged as the National League's leading hitter for the second straight season with a .339 average as a result of his late surge which included four hits in four at bats on the season's final day. Burris was mired in an ineffective year with a 4-11 record when he suddenly caught fire. He won 11 of his last 13 decisions, pitching four shutouts in his last 17 starts, to finish with a team-leading 15-13 record. Rick Reuschel was 14-12. On May 8 young Bruce Sutter was called up from the minors and immediately became a bullpen star, posting a 6-3 record.

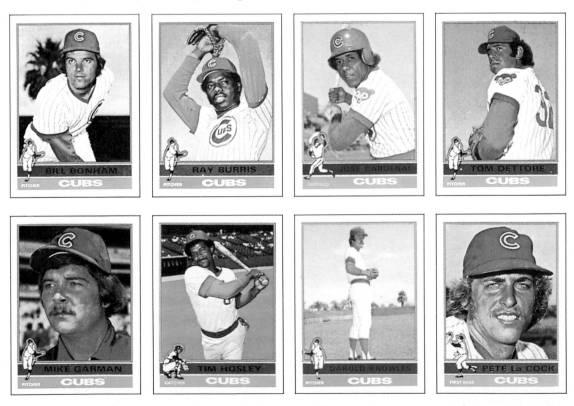

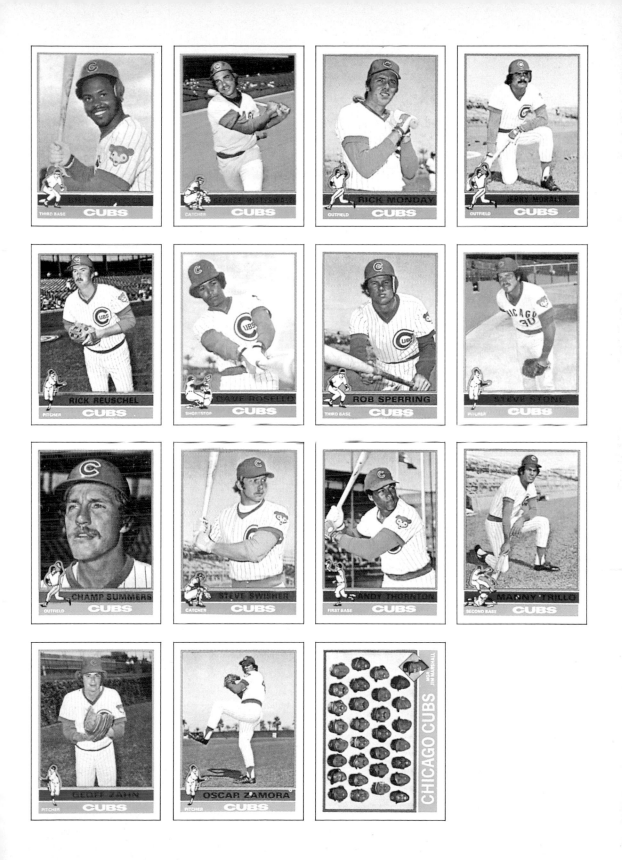

1977

Jim Marshall did not return to manage the Cubs in 1977. Instead, the team was under the direction of 63-year-old Herman Franks. Among the missing in spring was Bill Madlock, the Cubs first two-time batting champion since Cap Anson in 1887-88, who was traded to San Francisco for outfielder Bobby Murcer and third baseman Steve Ontiveros. In the first week of the season, the Cubs also lost their long-time owner. Philip K. Wrigley died at age 82 at Elkhorn, Wis., on April 12. His son, William, succeeded him as president, becoming the third Wrigley to head the Cubs.

Injuries to pitchers Bruce Sutter and Rick Reuschel played a major role. Sutter went 40 days without a save though his 31 were second best in the league. Reuschel was 15-3 when he was hurt on July 30 and finished 20-10. Murcer pounded out 27 home runs and had 89 RBIs while Ontiveros hit .299, although Greg Gross led the team with a .322 average in 115 games. By losing 8 of the last 9, the Cubs finished at .500 (81-81).

1978

Although they won two fewer games than the previous season, the Cubs managed to stay in the race in the National League East until mid-September before finally settling into third place with a 79-83 record. During the season the team spent 30 days in first place. One of the reasons for the excitement was the arrival of big Dave Kingman, a free-agent signee. Kingman had hit 176 home runs in 798 career games with five teams. While the Cubs' total of 72 homers was the lowest for the team since 1947, Kingman hit 28 and drove in 79 runs. Murcer slipped from 27 homers to nine. Speed also became a factor in the attack with 110 stolen bases being the most since 1923. Ivan DeJesus had a club-high 41, Rodney Scott 27 and Murcer 14. Starting pitching was a sparse commodity as Rick Reuschel (14-15) again led the team in wins.

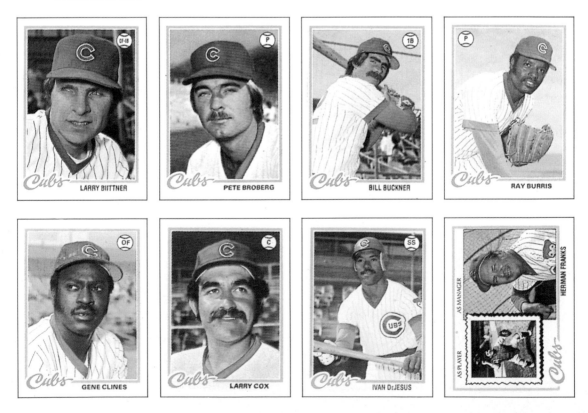

LARRY BIITTNER

PETE BROBERG

BILL BUCKNER

RAY BURRIS

GENE CLINES

LARRY COX

IVAN DeJESUS

HERMAN FRANKS

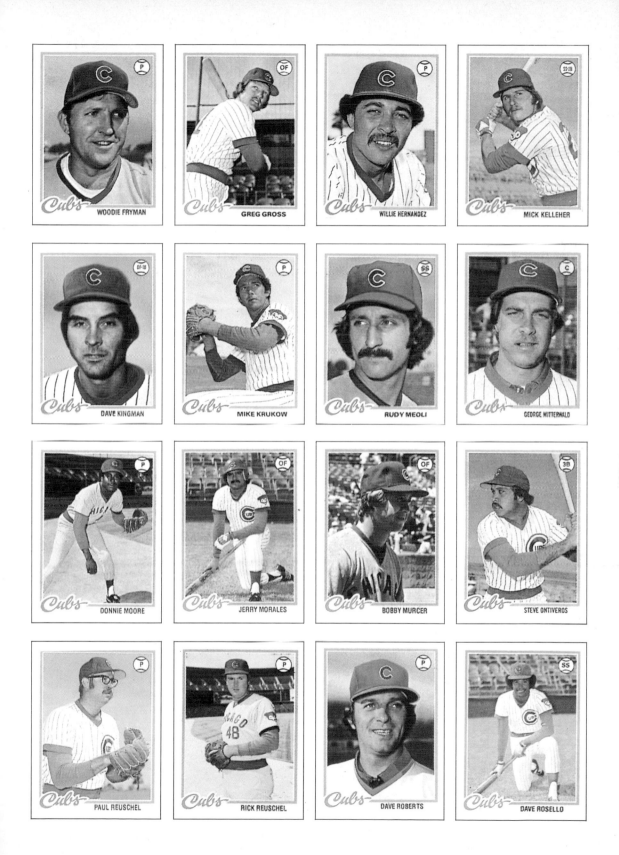

WOODIE FRYMAN

GREG GROSS

WILLIE HERNANDEZ

MICK KELLEHER

DAVE KINGMAN

MIKE KRUKOW

RUDY MEOLI

GEORGE MITTERWALD

DONNIE MOORE

JERRY MORALES

BOBBY MURCER

STEVE ONTIVEROS

PAUL REUSCHEL

RICK REUSCHEL

DAVE ROBERTS

DAVE ROSELLO

BRUCE SUTTER

STEVE SWISHER

MANNY TRILLO

JOE WALLIS

1979

It was the year of Dave Kingman at Wrigley Field. Enjoying easily his finest all-around season, the gangly (and often moody) slugger walloped 48 home runs, drove in 115 runs and batted .288 with 97 runs scored. He led the league in homers and slugging percentage (.613) and was second in RBIs while the batting average was the highest of his career.

The goofy game of May 17 was a microcosm of the season. The Cubs fell behind the Philadelphia Phillies, 17-6, but rallied implausibly behind Kingman's big bat to tie before finally losing, 23-22. Kingman hit three home runs and drove in six runs. The club ended with an 80-82 record, fifth in the division (18 games out). So frustrated was he by the performance that the 65-year-old Herman Franks quit in disgust in the final week; coach Joey Amalfitano managed the team as it lost five of the final seven. By failing to win the pennant, the Cubs matched the league record for years between flags (34), set by the old Boston Braves (1914 – 48).

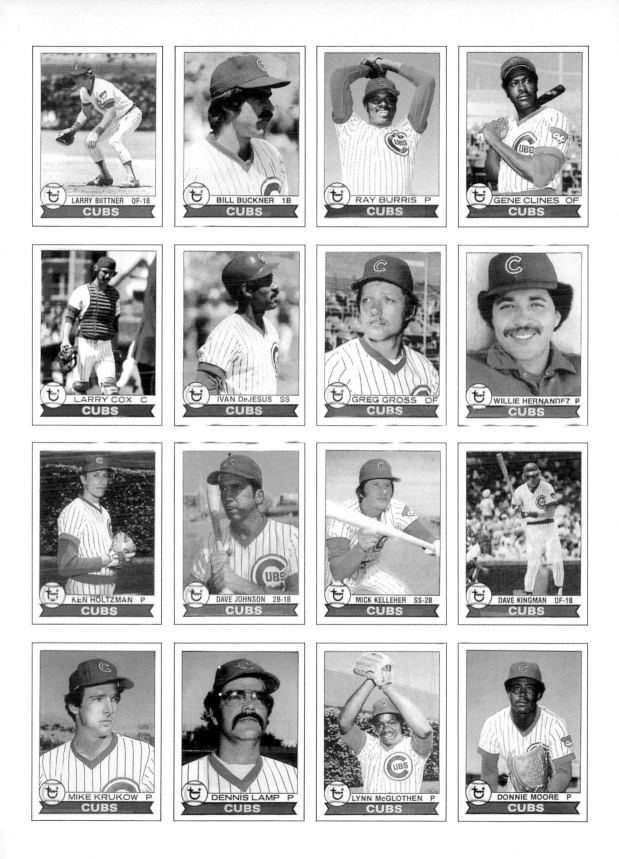

LARRY BIITTNER OF-1B	BILL BUCKNER 1B	RAY BURRIS P	GENE CLINES OF
CUBS	CUBS	CUBS	CUBS
LARRY COX C	IVAN DeJESUS SS	GREG GROSS OF	WILLIE HERNANDEZ P
CUBS	CUBS	CUBS	CUBS
KEN HOLTZMAN P	DAVE JOHNSON 2B-1B	MICK KELLEHER SS-2B	DAVE KINGMAN OF-1B
CUBS	CUBS	CUBS	CUBS
MIKE KRUKOW P	DENNIS LAMP P	LYNN McGLOTHEN P	DONNIE MOORE P
CUBS	CUBS	CUBS	CUBS

BOBBY MURCER OF
CUBS

STEVE ONTIVEROS 3B
CUBS

DAVE RADER C
CUBS

RICK REUSCHEL P
CUBS

DAVE ROBERTS P
CUBS

RODNEY SCOTT 3B-SS
CUBS

BRUCE SUTTER P
CUBS

MANNY TRILLO 2B
CUBS

MIKE VAIL OF
CUBS

JERRY WHITE OF
CUBS

1979 PROSPECTS
CUBS
DAVE GEISEL PITCHER
KARL PAGEL OUTFIELD
SCOT THOMPSON 1B-OF

CUBS
HERMAN FRANKS MANAGER

1980

When you combined the tenth-best team batting average with the eleventh-best team earned run average, the result is not a good record in a 12-team league, and that was the story of the Cubs in 1980. One of the great ironies of the season was that although the team hit only .251 overall, Bill Buckner was the batting champion. Buckner hit .324 to become the third Cubs player since 1972 to lead the league in hitting. Cubs batters had won four of the last nine titles. After having flirted with .500 the previous season, the Cubs collapsed to a 64-98 mark, finishing sixth in the East. Although coach Joey Amalfitano filled in after Herman Franks resigned during the last week of the 1979 season, Preston Gomez was named as the manager for 1980. After 90 games the Cubs were 38-52 and dead last. Gomez was fired and, once more, Amalfitano was named manager. His record was even worse (26-46) than Gomez's but, oddly, he was installed as the manager for 1981 as well.

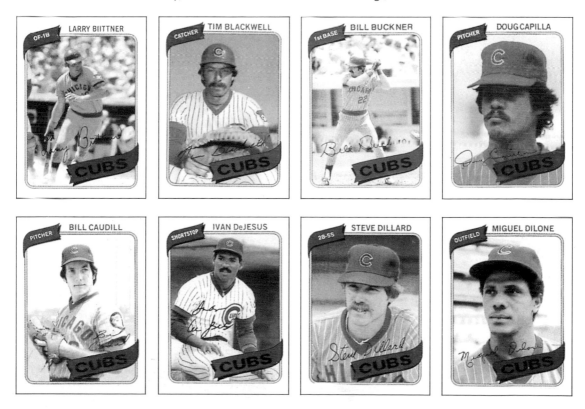

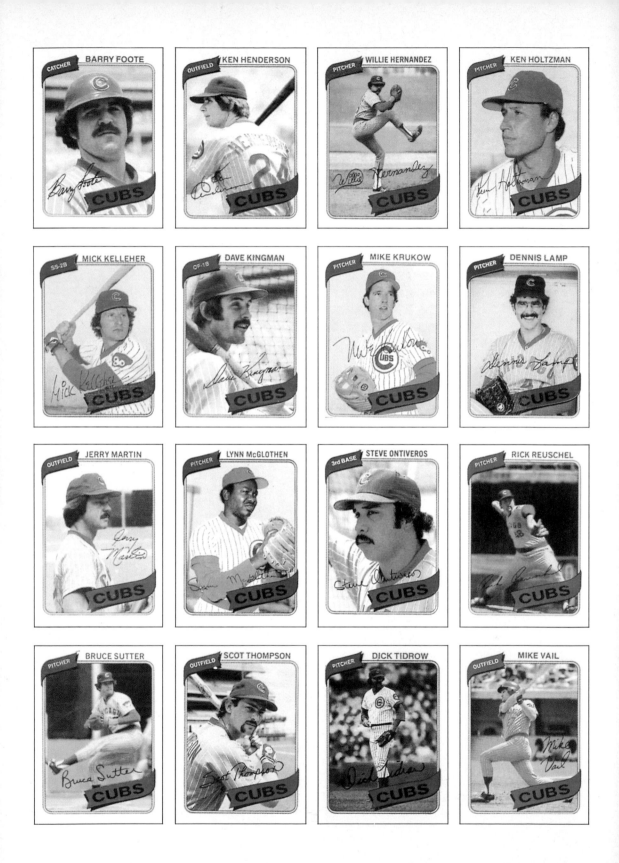

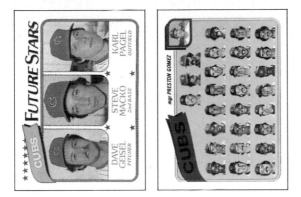

1981

One of the most unusual seasons in baseball history turned out to be absolutely wild for the Cubs. Even before the season opened, things started to happen. Dave Kingman, the home run champion of the league two years before, was traded to the New York Mets on the first day of spring training. By June 12 the Cubs had a 15-37 record, the worst of any team in the league, but the season came to a sudden and unscheduled halt when the players' union called a strike. Then, on June 16, came the biggest news of all. William Wrigley announced the sale of the team to *The Chicago Tribune* for $20.5 million, ending 66 years of control by the Wrigley family. When the season resumed, on Aug. 9, the Cubs were another team. In contrast to the 2-13 start to open the season, the Cubs started well and stayed in the race until five days remained in the second half of the split season, finishing with a 23-28 record (38-65 overall, 58 cancelled by the strike and one not made up).

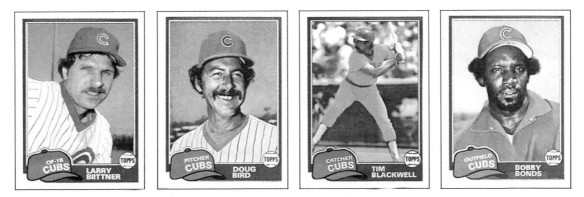

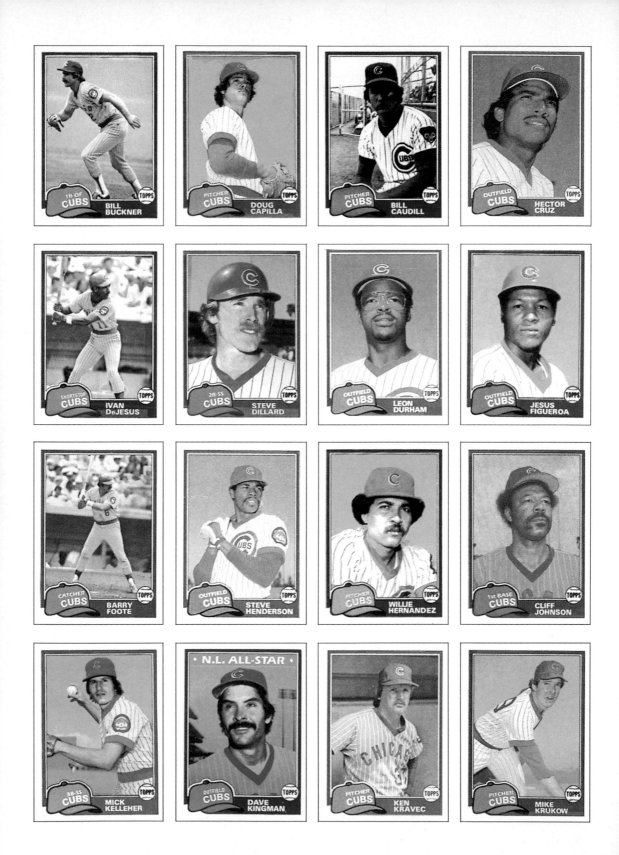

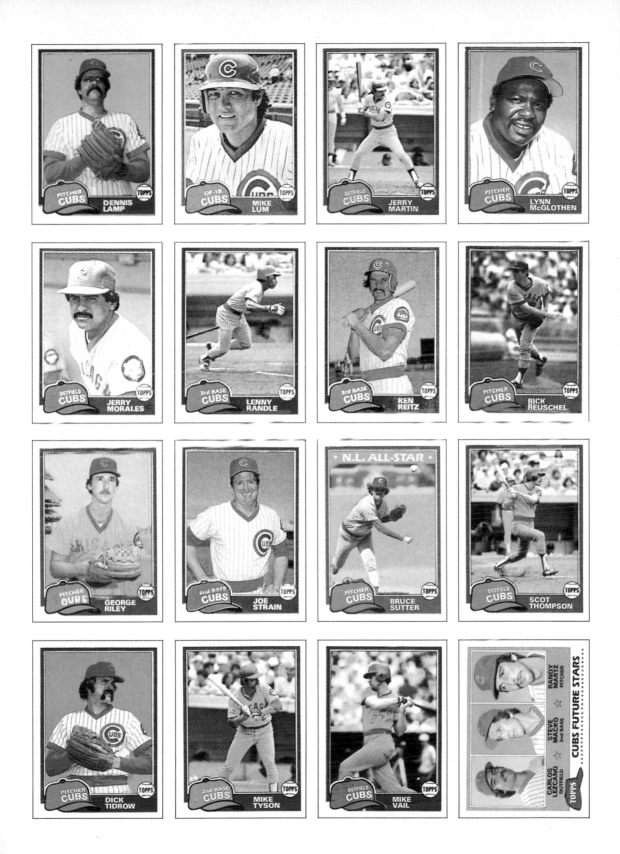

1982

With the new ownership came a whole new front office and field management team with former Phillies manager Dallas Green named general manager and his choice, Lee Elia, succeeding Joey Amalfitano as the manager. However, the season looked a lot like many of its predecessors. On May 30 a 13-game losing streak started, and by the end of June the record was 29-48. To make matters worse, the Cubs lost their final eight games in July en route to a 73-89 record for the season, placing the team fifth in the division, 19 games out of first. Leon Durham, obtained in the trade for Bruce Sutter, began to flower as a hitter, batting .312 with 22 homers and 90 RBIs. One of Dallas Green's first moves was to send shortstop Ivan DeJesus to Philadelphia for veteran Larry Bowa and young Ryne Sandberg who was installed at third base. Sandberg started 1-for-31 as a hitter but then took off and wound up hitting .271.

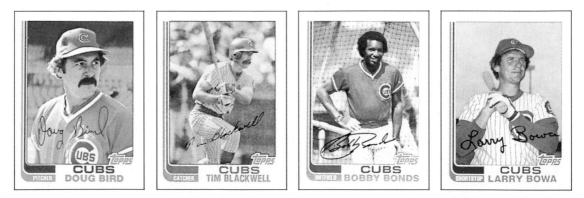

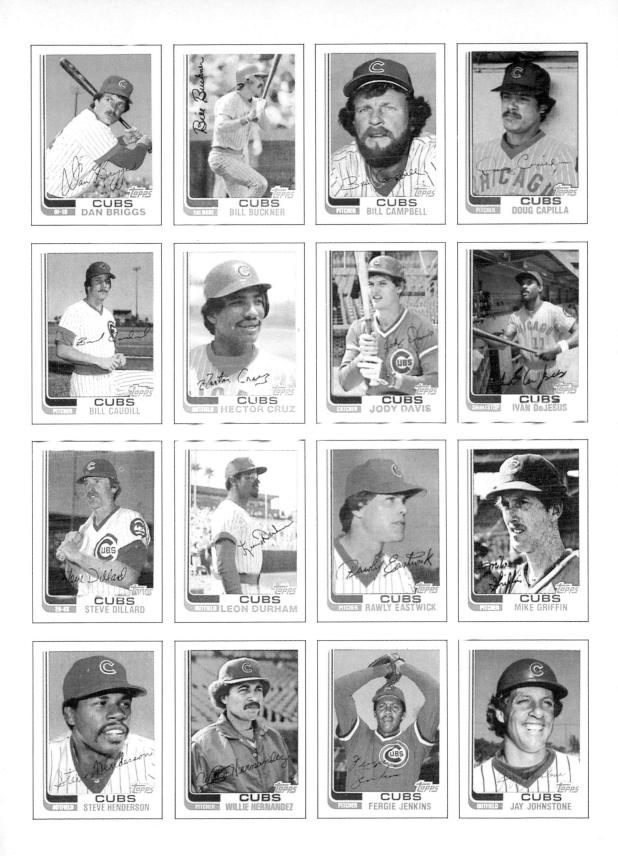

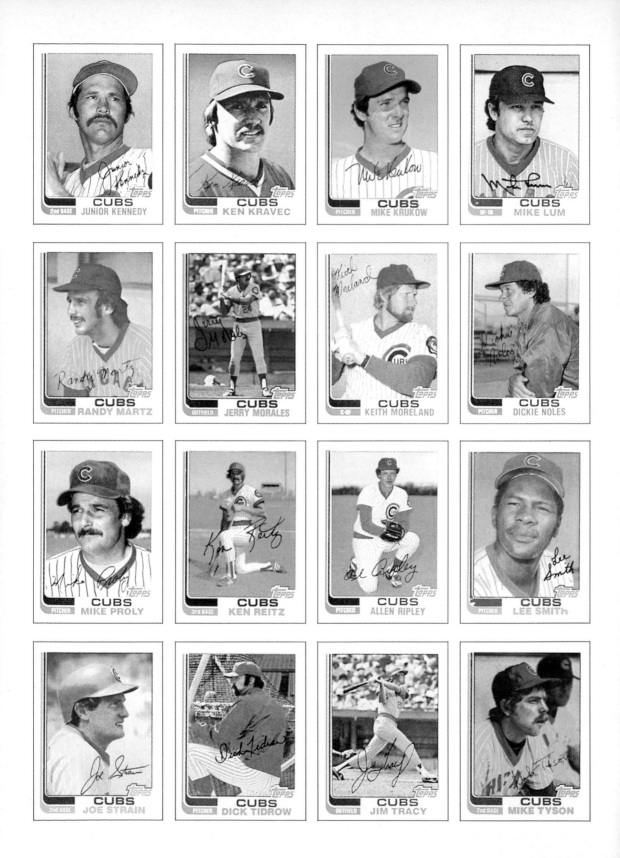

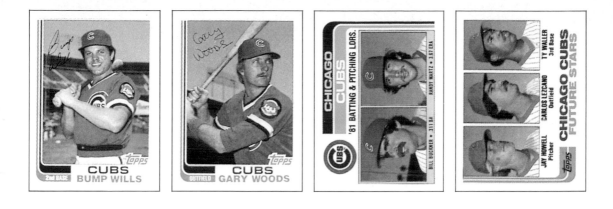

1983

After opening with six straight losses, the Cubs regrouped and appeared to become a factor in the National League East. The team opened June with seven wins in a row and by July 3 had climbed to 38-39 and was within two games of first place. Having won the first three games of a five-game series against Montreal, the Cubs lost both ends of the July 4 doubleheader, 6-3 and 4-2, before 39,394 at Wrigley Field. From then on, the team went into a skid, and by Aug. 22 the Cubs were 54-69, 10½ games out. Lee Elia was dismissed and Charlie Fox brought in from the front office to complete the season. Under Fox the Cubs were 17-22 to finish 71-91, fifth in the division. Ron Cey, a former Dodger, was the power leader with 24 home runs and 90 RBIs while hitting .275, and catcher Jody Davis (.271) also had 24 homers and added 84 RBIs. Chuck Rainey (14-13) was the top pitcher.

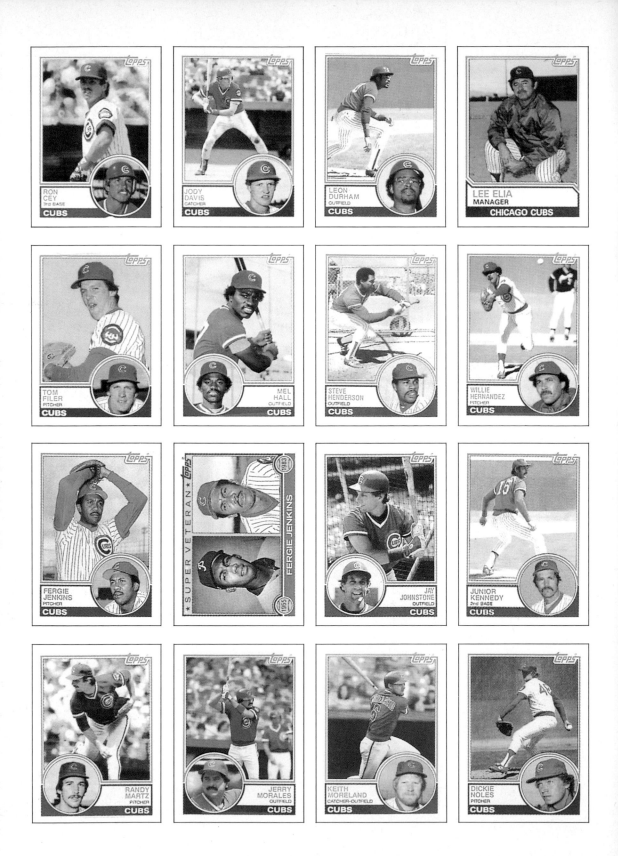

1984

Sparked by season-long superb performances from second baseman Ryne Sandberg and relief pitcher Lee Smith, the Cubs roared into first place in the National League East. They clinched the division on Sept. 24 with a 4-1 win at Pittsburgh. Rick Sutcliffe was the winning pitcher in the clinching game and his acquisition from Cleveland (where he was only 4-5) was the key to the entire season. Sutcliffe was an amazing 16-1 in 20 starts for the Cubs and won the N.L. Cy Young Award. Sandberg hit .314, was one of six Cubs with 80 or more RBIs (84), hit 19 homers and became only the fifth Cubs player to win the Most Valuable Player Award and the first since 1959. First-year manager Jim Frey was the manager of the year for the team's 96-65 record, which produced a 6 ½ -game final margin. Smith was 9-7 but second in the league in saves (33). Unfortunately, the San Diego Padres eliminated the Cubs, 3 games to 2, in the championship series for the pennant.

CUBS — CHUCK RAINEY P

CUBS — DICK RUTHVEN P

CUBS — RYNE SANDBERG 2B

CUBS — SCOTT SANDERSON P

CUBS — LEE SMITH P

CUBS — TIM STODDARD P

CUBS — RICK SUTCLIFFE P

CUBS — STEVE TROUT P

CUBS — TOM VERYZER SS-2B

CUBS — GARY WOODS OF

CUBS — BATTING & PITCHING LEADERS — FERGIE JENKINS 4.30 ERA — KEITH MORELAND .302 BA

1985

As the defending champions of the National League East, much was expected of the Cubs, who delivered a 77-84, fourth-place season. Much of the disappointment came about through an extraordinary rash of injuries. The four regular pitchers (Rick Sutcliffe, Dennis Eckersley, Steve Trout, Scott Sanderson) missed 52 starts during the season owing to injury, and after the All-Star break the regulars were available for only 27 of 72 starts. By season's end, Eckersley (11-7) was the only one of the 20 pitchers who worked during the season to win more than nine games although reliever Lee Smith (7-4) had another sterling season, finishing second in the league in saves (33). Ryne Sandberg also had another outstanding year, batting .305 with 26 homers and 83 RBIs, only slightly off the Most Valuable Player pace of the season before. Keith Moreland led the club with a .307 average and 106 RBIs with 14 homers.

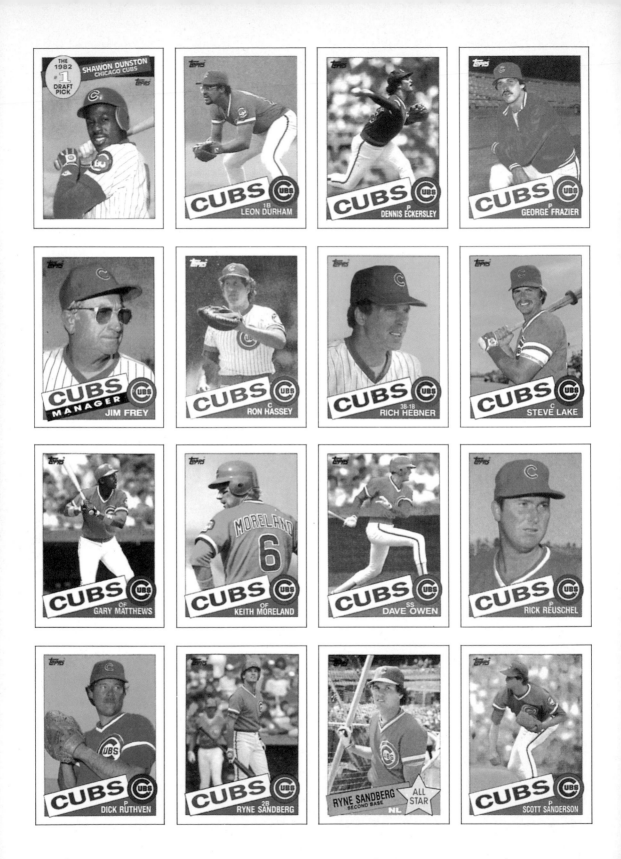

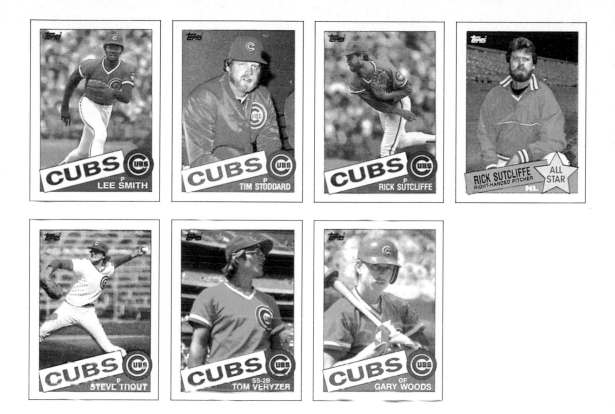

1986

Accumulating their worst full-season record since 1980, the Cubs fired Jim Frey, Manager of the Year just two years before, wound up 37 games behind division-leading New York and finished the season in chaos. Frey was fired June 12 with the club 23-33. He was replaced by former Yankees skipper Gene Michael who guided the team to a 46-56 record and a 70-90 finish in fifth place.

On May 1, thanks to the Mets' hot start, the Cubs were 7 games out with a 7-11 record. Two days later, Ron Cey hit his 300th career home run, becoming only the fifth third baseman to reach that plateau. Jody Davis (.250) and Gary Matthews (.259) shared the club homer lead with 21 each while Keith Moreland (.271, 12 homers) was the RBI leader with 79. Cey, limited to 97 games by injuries, finished with 13 homers but only 36 RBIs. Just one pitcher (Scott Sanderson, 9-11) had more than 7 wins among the starters. Lee Smith (9-9) led the relievers with 31 of the team total of 42 saves.

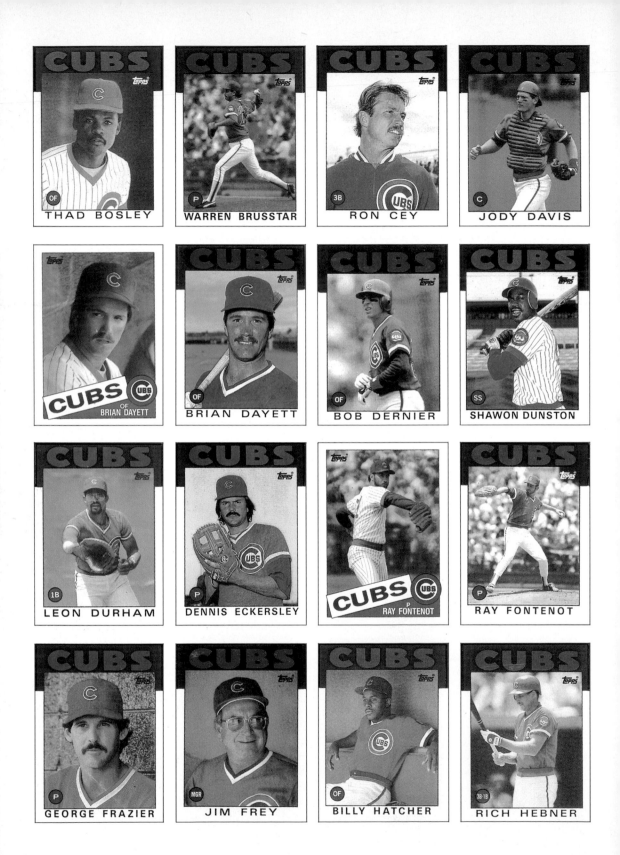

THAD BOSLEY

WARREN BRUSSTAR

RON CEY

JODY DAVIS

BRIAN DAYETT

BRIAN DAYETT

BOB DERNIER

SHAWON DUNSTON

LEON DURHAM

DENNIS ECKERSLEY

RAY FONTENOT

RAY FONTENOT

GEORGE FRAZIER

JIM FREY

BILLY HATCHER

RICH HEBNER

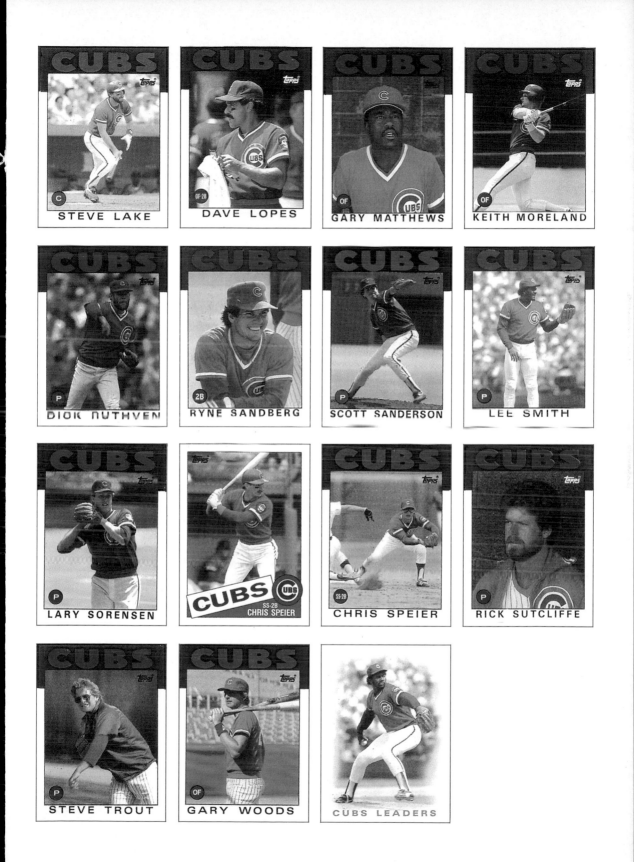

STEVE LAKE

DAVE LOPES

GARY MATTHEWS

KEITH MORELAND

DICK RUTHVEN

RYNE SANDBERG

SCOTT SANDERSON

LEE SMITH

LARY SORENSEN

CUBS
SS-2B
CHRIS SPEIER

CHRIS SPEIER

RICK SUTCLIFFE

STEVE TROUT

GARY WOODS

CUBS LEADERS

1987

Even a .264 batting average, plus a club-record and league-leading 209 home runs were insufficient when it came to keeping the Cubs out of the National League East basement last year. It was pitching or, rather, the lack of it that doomed the Bruins.

The rebounding Rick Sutcliffe led the league with 18 wins and gained the Cy Young Award, but his mound confreres couldn't approach the big righthander's numbers. Except for rookie Les Lancaster, whose 4.90 ERA belied his 8-3 record, no other Cubs moundsman had a winning record. As usual, veteran bullpenner Lee Smith performed well, registering 36 saves. But no other reliever had as many as five.

Offensively, Andre Dawson helped ease the club's 85 losses. The free agent signee won the MVP with his league-leading 49 home runs and his 137 RBIs. Veteran switchhitter Jerry Mumphrey was one who abetted Dawson, hitting .333, while Bob Dernier, though platooned in the outfield, stroked .317 in 93 games.

Ryne Sandberg and Manny Trillo each batted .294, while first baseman Leon Durham and full-time third baseman Keith Moreland each contributed 27 home runs. Shawon Dunston, the highly touted young shortstop, was limited to only 95 appearances because of a broken hand that sidelined him for three months.

SCOTT SANDERSON

LEE SMITH

CHRIS SPEIER

JIM SUNDBERG

RICK SUTCLIFFE

MANNY TRILLO

STEVE TROUT

CHICO WALKER

CUBS LEADERS

1988

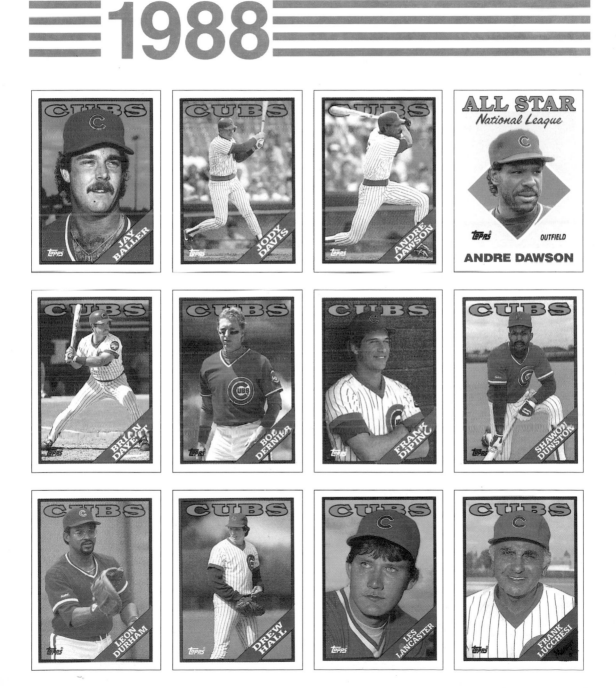

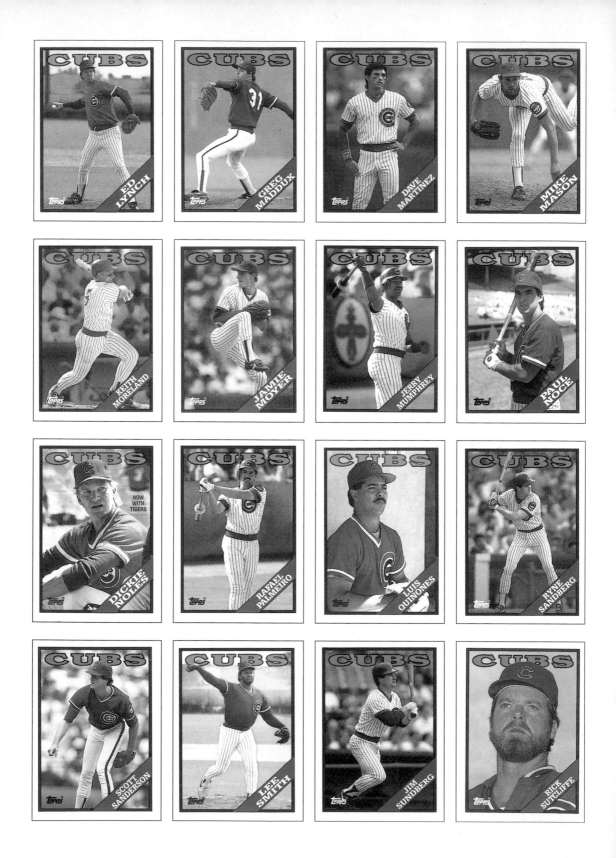

1951: Blue Back of Johnny Mize (50) lists for $25 . . . Red Back of Duke Snider (38) lists for $18 . . . Complete set of 9 Team Cards lists for $900 . . . Complete set of 11 Connie Mack All-Stars lists for $2750 with Babe Ruth and Lou Gehrig listing for $700 each . . . Current All-Stars of Jim Konstanty, Robin Roberts and Eddie Stanky list for $4000 each . . . Complete set lists for $14,250.

1952: Mickey Mantle (311) is unquestionably the most sought-after post-war gum card, reportedly valued at $6,500-plus . . . Ben Chapman (391) is photo of Sam Chapman . . . Complete set lists in excess of $36,000.

1953: Mickey Mantle (82) and Willie Mays (244) list for $1,500 each . . . Set features first TOPPS card of Hall-of-Famer Whitey Ford (207) and only TOPPS card of Hall-of-Famer Satchel Paige (220). Pete Runnels (219) is photo of Don Johnson . . . Complete set lists for $9,500.

1954: Ted Williams is depicted on two cards (1 and 250) . . . Set features rookie cards of Hank Aaron (128), Ernie Banks (94) and Al Kaline (201) . . . Card of Aaron lists for $650 . . . Card of Willie Mays (90) lists for $200 . . . Complete set lists for $5,500.

1955: Set features rookie cards of Sandy Koufax (123), Harmon Killebrew (124) and Roberto Clemente (164) . . . The Clemente and Willie Mays (194) cards list for $425 each . . .Complete set lists for $3,900.

1956: Set features rookie cards of Hall-of-Famers Will Harridge (1), Warren Giles (2), Walter Alston (8) and Luis Aparicio (292) . . . Card of Mickey Mantle (135) lists for $650 . . . Card of Willie Mays (130) lists for $125 . . . Complete set lists for $4,000 . . . The Team Cards are found both dated (1955) and undated and are valued at $15 (dated) and more . . . There are two unnumbered Checklist Cards valued high.

1957: Set features rookie cards of Don Drysdale (18), Frank Robinson (35) and Brooks Robinson (328) . . . A reversal of photo negative made Hank Aaron (20) appear as a left-handed batter . . . Card of Mickey Mantle (95) lists for $600 . . . Cards of Brooks Robinson and Sandy Koufax (302) list for $275 each . . . Complete set lists for $4,800.

1958: Set features first TOPPS cards of Casey Stengel (475) and Stan Musial (476) . . . Mike McCormick (37) is photo of Ray Monzant . . . Milt Bolling (188) is photo of Lou Berberet . . . Bob Smith (226) is photo of Bobby Gene Smith . . . Card of Mickey Mantle (150) lists for $400 . . . Card of Ted Williams (1) lists for $325 . . . Complete set lists for $4,800.

1959: In a notable error, Lou Burdette (440) is shown posing as a left-handed pitcher . . . Set features rookie card of Bob Gibson (514) . . . Ralph Lumenti (316) is photo of Camilo Pascual . . . Card of Gibson lists for $200 . . . Card of Mickey Mantle (10) lists for $300 . . . Complete set lists for $3,000.

1960: A run of 32 consecutively numbered rookie cards (117-148) includes the first card of Carl Yastrzemski (148) . . . J.C. Martin (346) is photo of Gary Peters . . . Gary Peters (407) is photo of J.C. Martin . . . Card of Yastrzemski lists for $150 . . . Card of Mickey Mantle (350) lists for $300 . . . Complete set lists for $2,600.

1961: The Warren Spahn All-Star (589) should have been numbered 587 . . . Set features rookie cards of Billy Williams (141) and Juan Marichal (417) . . . Dutch Dotterer (332) is photo of his brother, Tommy . . . Card of Mickey Mantle (300) lists for $200 . . . Card of Carl Yastrzemski (287) lists for $90 . . . Complete set lists for $3,600.

1962: Set includes special Babe Ruth feature (135-144) . . . some Hal Reniff cards numbered 139 should be 159 . . . Set features rookie card of Lou Brock (387) . . . Gene Freese (205) is shown posing as a left-handed batter . . . Card of Mickey Mantle (200) lists for $325 . . . Card of Carl Yastrzemski (425) lists for $125 . . . Complete set lists for $3,300.

1963: Set features rookie card of Pete Rose (537), which lists for $500-plus . . . Bob Uecker (126) is shown posing as a left-handed batter . . . Don Landrum (113) is photo of Ron Santo . . . Eli Grba (231) is photo of Ryne Duren . . . Card of Mickey Mantle (200) lists for $200 . . . Card of Lou Brock (472) lists for $75 . . . Complete set lists for $2,900.

1964: Set features rookie cards of Richie Allen (243), Tony Conigliaro (287) and Phil Niekro (541) . . . Lou Burdette is again shown posing as a left-handed pitcher . . . Bud Bloomfield (532) is photo of Jay Ward . . . Card of Pete Rose (125) lists for $150 . . . Card of Mickey Mantle (50) lists for $175 . . . Complete set lists for $1,600.

1965: Set features rookie cards of Dave Johnson (473), Steve Carlton (477) and Jim Hunter (526) . . . Lew Krausse (462) is photo of Pete Lovrich . . . Gene Freese (492) is again shown posing as a left-handed batter . . . Cards of Carlton and Pete Rose (207) list for $135 . . . Card of Mickey Mantle (350) lists for $300 . . . Complete set lists for $800.

1966: Set features rookie card of Jim Palmer (126) . . . For the third time (see 1962 and 1965) Gene Freese (319) is shown posing as a left-handed batter . . . Dick Ellsworth (447) is photo of Ken Hubbs (died February 13, 1964) . . . Card of Gaylord Perry (598) lists for $175 . . . Card of Willie McCovey (550) lists for $80 . . . Complete set lists for $2,500.

1967: Set features rookie cards of Rod Carew (569) and Tom Seaver (581) . . . Jim Fregosi (385) is shown posing as a left-handed batter . . . George Korince (72) is photo of James Brown but was later corrected on a second Korince card (526) . . . Card of Carew lists for $150 . . . Card of Maury Wills (570) lists for $65 . . . Complete set lists for $2,500.

1968: Set features rookie cards of Nolan Ryan (177) and Johnny Bench (247) . . . The special feature of The Sporting News All-Stars (361-380) includes eight players in the Hall of Fame . . . Card of Ryan lists for $135 . . . Card of Bench lists for $125 . . . Complete set lists for $1,200.

1969: Set features rookie card of Reggie Jackson (260) . . . There are two poses each for Clay Dalrymple (151) and Donn Clendenon (208) . . . Aurelio Rodriguez (653) is photo of Lenny Garcia (Angels' bat boy) . . . Card of Mickey Mantle (500) lists for $150 . . . Card of Jackson lists for $175 . . . Complete set lists for $1,200.

1970: Set features rookie cards of Vida Blue (21), Thurman Munson (189) and Bill Buckner (286) . . . Also included are two deceased players Miguel Fuentes (88) and Paul Edmondson (414) who died after cards went to press . . . Card of Johnny Bench (660) lists for $75 . . . Card of Pete Rose (580) lists for $75 . . . Complete set lists for $1,000.

1971: Set features rookie card of Steve Garvey (341) . . . the final series (644-752) is found in lesser quantity and includes rookie card (664) of three pitchers named Reynolds (Archie, Bob and Ken) . . . Card of Garvey lists for $65 . . . Card of Pete Rose (100) lists for $45 . . . Complete set lists for $1,000.

1972: There were 16 cards featuring photos of players in their boyhood years . . . Dave Roberts (91) is photo of Danny Coombs . . . Brewers Rookie Card (162) includes photos of Darrell Porter and Jerry Bell, which were reversed . . . Cards of Steve Garvey (686) and Rod Carew (695) list for $60 . . . Card of Pete Rose (559) lists for $50 . . . Complete set lists for $1,000.

1973: A special Home Run Card (1) depicted Babe Ruth, Hank Aaron and Willie Mays . . . Set features rookie card of Mike Schmidt (615) listing for $175 . . . Joe Rudi (360) is photo of Gene Tenace . . . Card of Pete Rose (130) lists for $18 . . . Card of Reggie Jackson (255) lists for $12.50 . . . Complete set lists for $600.

1974: Set features 15 San Diego Padres cards printed as "Washington, N.L." due to report of franchise move, later corrected . . . Also included was a 44-card Traded Series which updated team changes . . . Set features rookie card of Dave Winfield (456) . . . Card of Mike Schmidt (283) lists for $35 . . . Card of Winfield lists for $25 . . . Complete set lists for $325.

1975: Herb Washington (407) is the only card ever published with position "designated runner," featuring only base-running statistics . . . Set features rookie cards of Robin Yount (223), George Brett (228), Jim Rice (616), Gary Carter (620) and Keith Hernandez (623) . . . Don Wilson (455) died after cards went to press (January 5, 1975) . . . Card of Brett lists for $50 . . . Cards of Rice and Carter list for $35 . . . Complete set lists for $475 . . . TOPPS also tested the complete 660-card series in a smaller size (2¼" x 3 1/8") in certain areas of USA in a limited supply . . . Complete set of "Mini-Cards" lists for $700.

1976: As in 1974 there was a 44-card Traded Series . . . Set features five Father & Son cards (66-70) and ten All-Time All-Stars (341-350) . . . Card of Pete Rose (240) lists for $15 . . . Cards of Jim Rice (340), Gary Carter (441) and George Brett (19) list for $12 . . . Complete set lists for $225.

1977: Set features rookie cards of Andre Dawson (473) and Dale Murphy (476) . . . Reuschel Brother Combination (634) shows the two (Paul and Rick) misidentified . . . Dave Collins (431) is photo of Bob Jones . . . Card of Murphy lists for $65 . . . Card of Pete Rose (450) lists for $8.50 . . . Complete set lists for $250.

1978: Record Breakers (1-7) feature Lou Brock, Sparky Lyle, Willie McCovey, Brooks Robinson, Pete Rose, Nolan Ryan and Reggie Jackson . . . Set features rookie cards of Jack Morris (703), Lou Whitaker (704), Paul Molitor/Alan Trammell (707), Lance Parrish (708) and Eddie Murray (36) . . . Card of Murray lists for $35 . . . Card of Parrish lists for $35 . . . Complete set lists for $200.

1979: Bump Wills (369) was originally shown with Blue Jays affiliation but later corrected to Rangers . . . Set features rookie cards of Ozzie Smith (116), Pedro Guerrero (719), Lonnie Smith (722) and Terry Kennedy (724) . . . Larry Cox (489) is photo of Dave Rader . . . Card of Dale Murphy (39) lists for $8 . . . Cards of Ozzie Smith and Eddie Murray (640) list for $7.50 . . . Complete set lists for $135.

1980: Highlights (1-6) feature Hall-of-Famers Lou Brock, Carl Yastrzemski, Willie McCovey and Pete Rose . . . Set features rookie cards of Dave Stieb (77), Rickey Henderson (482) and Dan Quisenberry (667) . . . Card of Henderson lists for $28 . . . Card of Dale Murphy (274) lists for $5.50 . . . Complete set lists for $135.

1981: Set features rookie cards of Fernando Valenzuela (302), Kirk Gibson (315), Harold Baines (347) and Tim Raines (479) . . . Jeff Cox (133) is photo of Steve McCatty . . . John Littlefield (489) is photo of Mark Riggins . . . Card of Valenzuela lists for $7.50 . . . Card of Raines lists for $9 . . . Complete set lists for $80.

1982: Pascual Perez (383) printed with no position on front lists for $36, later corrected . . . Set features rookie cards of Cal Ripken (21), Jesse Barfield (203), Steve Sax (681) and Kent Hrbek (766) . . . Dave Rucker (261) is photo of Roger Weaver . . . Steve Bedrosian (502) is photo of Larry Owen . . . Card of Ripken lists for $12.50 . . . Cards of Barfield and Sax list for $5 . . . Complete set lists for $75.

1983: Record Breakers (1-6) feature Tony Armas, Rickey Henderson, Greg Minton, Lance Parrish, Manny Trillo and John Wathan . . . A series of Super Veterans features early and current photos of 34 leading players . . . Set features rookie cards of Tony Gwynn (482) and Wade Boggs (498) . . . Card of Boggs lists for $32 . . . Card of Gwynn lists for $16 . . . Complete set lists for $85.

1984: Highlights (1-6) salute eleven different players . . . A parade of superstars is included in Active Leaders (701-718) . . . Set features rookie card of Don Mattingly (8) listing for $35 . . . Card of Darryl Strawberry (182) lists for $10 . . . Complete set lists for $85.

1985: A Father & Son Feature (131-143) is again included . . . Set features rookie cards of Scott Bankhead (393), Mike Dunne (395), Shane Mack (398), John Marzano (399), Oddibe McDowell (400), Mark McGwire (401), Pat Pacillo (402), Cory Snyder (403) and Billy Swift (404) as part of salute to 1984 USA Baseball Team (389-404) that participated in Olympic Games plus rookie cards of Roger Clemens (181) and Eric Davis (627) . . . Card of McGwire lists for $20 . . . Card of Davis lists for $18 . . . Card of Clemens lists for $11 . . . Complete set lists for $95.

1986: Set includes Pete Rose Feature (2-7), which reproduces each of Rose's TOPPS cards from 1963 thru 1985 (four per card) . . . Bob Rodgers (141) should have been numbered 171 . . . Ryne Sandberg (690) is the only card with TOPPS logo omitted . . . Complete set lists for $24.

1987: Record Breakers (1-7) feature Roger Clemens, Jim Deshaies, Dwight Evans, Davey Lopes, Dave Righetti, Ruben Sierra and Todd Worrell . . . Jim Gantner (108) is shown with Brewers logo reversed . . . Complete set lists for $22.

1988: Record Breakers (1-7) include Vince Coleman, Don Mattingly, Mark McGwire, Eddie Murray, Phil & Joe Niekro, Nolan Ryan and Benny Santiago. Al Leiter (18) was originally shown with photo of minor leaguer Steve George and later corrected. Complete set lists for $20.00.

Pitching Record & Index

PLAYER	G	IP	W	L	R	ER	SO	BB	GS	CG	SHO	SV	ERA
ABERNATHY, TED	681	1148	63	69			765	592	34	7	2	148	3.46
ADAMS, RED	8	12	0	1			8	7	0	0	0	0	8.25
AGUIRRE, HANK	477	1376	75	72			856	479	149	44	9	33	3.24
AKER, JACK	495	746	47	45			404	274	0	0	0	123	3.28
ALTAMIRANO, PORFIRIO	65	91.2	7	4			57	30	0	0	0	2	4.03
ANDERSON, BOB	246	841	36	46			502	319	93	15	1	13	4.26
BARBER, STEVE	466	1998	121	106			1309	950	272	59	21	13	3.36
BAUMANN, FRANK	244	798	45	38			384	300	78	19	4	13	4.11
BEARD, DAVE	161	257.2	19	18			180	115	2	0	0	30	4.61
BIRD, DOUG	432	1213.2	73	60			680	296	100	8	3	60	3.99
BONHAM, BILL	300	1488	75	83			985	636	212	22	4	11	4.00
BORDI, RICH	155	330.2	17	18	162	147	218	104	14	0	0	4	4.00
BREWER, JIM	584	1044	69	65			810	360	35	1	0	132	3.06
BRIGGS, JOHNNY T.	59	166	9	11			80	82	21	3	1	1	4.99
BROBERG, PETE	206	963	41	71			536	478	134	26	6	1	4.56
BROGLIO, ERNIE	259	1337	77	74			849	587	184	52	18	2	3.74
BROSNAN, JIM	385	832	55	47			507	312	47	7	2	67	3.54
BRUSSTAR, WARREN	340	484.1	28	16			273	183	0	0	0	11	3.51
BRYANT, CLAY	129	542	32	20			272	262	45	23	4	7	3.74
BUHL, BOB	457	2587	166	132			1268	1105	369	111	20	6	3.55
BURDETTE, FREDDIE	30	35	1	1			10	20	0	0	0	0	3.34
BURDETTE, LEW	626	3068	203	144			1074	628	373	158	33	31	3.66
BURRIS, RAY	447	2083.2	102	127			1023	720	290	47	10	7	4.10
BUZHARDT, JOHN	326	1489	71	96			678	435	203	44	15	7	3.67
CALMUS, DICK	22	48	3	1			26	16	2	0	0	0	3.19
CAMPBELL, BILL	693	1219.2	83	68	538	475	860	491	9	2	1	126	3.51
CAPILLA, DOUG	136	293	12	18	162	141	166	147	31	1	0	2	4.33
CARDWELL, DON	410	2122	102	138			1211	671	301	72	17	7	3.92
CAUDILL, BILL	439	659.1	35	52	289	265	612	287	24	0	0	105	3.62
CECCARELLI, ART	79	307	9	18			166	147	42	8	3	0	5.04
CHAMBERS, CLIFF	189	897	48	53			374	361	113	37	6	1	4.29
CHIPMAN, BOB	293	880	51	46			322	386	87	29	7	14	3.72
CHURCH, BUBBA	147	713	36	37			274	277	95	32	7	4	4.10
COLBORN, JIM	301	1597	83	88			688	475	204	60	8	7	3.80
COLEMAN, JOE H.	484	2571	142	135			1728	1003	340	94	18	7	3.69
COLLUM, JACKIE	171	464	32	28			171	173	37	11	2	12	4.15
CONNORS, BILL	26	43	0	2			24	19	1	0	0	0	7.53
COSMAN, JIM	12	41	2	1			16	27	6	1	0	0	3.07
CROSBY, KEN	16	20	1	0			11	15	1	0	0	0	8.55
CULP, RAY	322	1897	122	101			1411	752	268	80	22	1	3.58
CURTIS, JACK	69	279	14	19			108	89	35	6	1	0	4.84
DAVIS, JIM	154	407	24	26			197	179	39	4	1	10	4.00
DECKER, JOE	152	710	36	44			455	377	106	19	4	0	4.17
DETTORE, TOM	68	180	8	11			106	78	15	0	0	0	5.20
DIPINO, FRANK	233	333.1	15	29			279	143	6	0	0	43	3.81
DISTASO, ALEC	2	5	0	0			1	1	0	0	0	0	3.60
DOWLING, DAVE	2	10	1	0			3	1	1	0	0	0	1.80
DRABOWSKY, MOE	589	1640	88	105			1162	702	154	30	6	55	3.71
DROTT, DICK	176	687	27	46			460	405	101	14	5	1	4.78
DUBIEL, WALT	187	880	45	53			289	349	97	41	9	11	3.87
DUNEGAN, JIM	7	13	0	2			5	6	0	0	0	0	4.85
EARLEY, ARNOLD	223	381	12	20			310	184	10	1	0	14	4.49
EASTWICK, RAWLY	326	526	28	27			295	156	1	0	0	68	3.30
ECKERSLEY, DENNIS	376	2496	151	128	1101	1018	1627	624	359	100	20	3	3.67

PLAYER	G	IP	W	L	R	ER	SO	BB	GS	CG	SHO	SV	ERA
ELLSWORTH, DICK	407	2156	115	137			1140	595	310	87	9	5	3.72
ELSTON, DON	450	755.2	49	54			519	327	15	2	0	63	3.69
ESTRADA, CHUCK	146	764	50	44			535	416	105	24	2	0	4.08
FAST, DARCY	8	10	0	1			10	8	0	0	0	2	5.40
FAUL, BILL	71	262	12	16			164	95	33	8	3	2	4.71
FILER, TOM	19	89.1	8	2			39	36	17	0	0	0	4.63
FODGE, GENE	16	40	1	1			15	11	4	0	0	0	4.73
FONTENOT, RAY	145	493.2	25	26	253	221	216	153	62	3	1	2	4.03
FRAILING, KEN	116	218	10	16			136	82	19	1	0	0	3.96
FRAZIER, GEORGE	361	594.1	30	38	300	270	391	262	0	0	0	27	4.09
FREEMAN, HERSHELL	204	360	30	16			158	109	3	1	0	37	3.73
FREEMAN, MARK	34	88	3	3			55	38	9	1	0	1	5.52
GARDNER, ROB	109	332	14	18			193	133	42	4	0	1	4.34
GARMAN, MIKE	303	434	22	27			213	202	8	0	0	42	3.63
GEISEL, DAVE	119	181.1	5	5			127	82	8	0	0	8	3.67
GIUSTI, DAVE	668	1718	100	93			1103	570	133	35	9	145	3.60
GRIFFIN, MIKE	41	124.1	4	10			58	37	18	0	0	2	4.49
GUMPERT, DAVE	78	116.1	3	2	61	52	63	44	1	0	0	5	4.02
GURA, LARRY	395	2022	126	94			792	590	257	71	16	13	3.69
HACKER, WARREN	306	1283	62	89			557	320	157	47	6	17	4.21
HAMILTON, STEVE	421	662	40	31			531	214	17	3	1	42	3.06
HANDS, BILL	374	1951	111	110			1098	492	260	72	17	14	3.35
HARGESHEIMER, ALAN	26	98	5	8			51	43	16	0	0	0	4.50
HARTENSTEIN, CHUCK	187	297	17	19			135	89	0	0	0	23	4.39
HATTEN, JOE	233	1087	65	49			381	492	149	51	7	4	3.87
HENDLEY, BOB	216	879	48	52			522	329	126	25	6	12	3.97
HENRY, BILL R.	527	914	46	50			619	296	44	12	0	90	3.51
HERNANDEZ, RAMON	337	432	23	15			255	135	0	0	0	46	3.02
HERNANDEZ, WILLIE	604	897	59	52	359	329	669	282	11	0	0	114	3.30
HILLER, FRANK	138	533	30	32			197	158	60	22	5	3	4.42
HILLMAN, DAVE	188	624	21	37			296	185	64	8	1	3	3.87
HOBBIE, GLEN	284	1263	62	81			682	495	170	45	11	6	4.20
HOEFT, BILLY	505	1848	97	101			1140	685	200	75	17	33	3.94
HOFFMAN, GUY	58	74	2	3			44	42	1	0	0	1	4.14
HOLTZMAN, KEN	451	2868	174	150			1601	910	410	127	31	3	3.49
HOOTON, BURT	480	2651.2	151	136			1491	799	377	86	29	7	3.38
HOWELL, JAY	202	390	26	26	184	172	312	146	21	2	0	52	3.97
HUGHES, JIM R.	172	297	15	13			165	152	1	0	0	39	3.82
HUMPHREYS, BOB	319	568	27	21			364	219	4	0	0	20	3.34
JACKSON, LARRY	558	3262	194	183			1709	824	429	149	37	20	3.40
JACOBS, TONY	2	4	0	0			3	3	0	0	0	0	11.25
JAECKEL, PAUL	4	3	1	0			2	3	0	0	0	1	0.00
JEFFCOAT, HAL	245	697	39	37			239	257	51	13	1	25	4.22
JENKINS, FERGIE	664	4498.2	284	226			3192	997	594	267	49	7	3.34
JOHNSON, BEN	21	46	2	1			15	15	4	0	0	0	3.91
JOHNSON, KEN	334	1736	91	106			1042	413	331	50	7	9	3.46
JONES, SAM	322	1644	102	101			1376	822	222	76	17	9	3.59
JONES, SHELDON	260	919	54	57			413	413	101	33	5	12	3.97
KAISER, DON	58	240	6	15			108	85	35	6	1	0	4.16
KELLY, BOB	123	362	12	18			146	152	35	7	2	4	4.50
KENNEDY, MONTE	249	960	42	55			411	495	127	48	6	4	3.84
KLIPPSTEIN, JOHNNY	711	1970	101	118			1158	978	162	37	6	66	4.24
KNOWLES, DAROLD	765	1091	66	74			681	480	8	1	0	143	3.12
KOONCE, CAL	334	972	47	49			504	368	90	9	3	24	3.78
KRAVEC, KEN	160	859	43	56			557	404	128	24	6	1	4.46

PLAYER	G	IP	W	L	R	ER	SO	BB	GS	CG	SHO	SV	ERA
KRUKOW, MIKE	311	1859.1	108	104	900	794	1281	672	299	37	10	1	3.84
LA ROCHE, DAVE	647	1049	65	58			819	459	15	7	3	126	3.53
LAMABE, JACK	285	710	33	41			434	238	49	7	3	15	4.25
LAMP, DENNIS	396	1353.2	74	76	670	587	590	411	157	21	7	33	3.90
LARSEN, DON	412	1549	81	91			849	725	171	44	11	23	3.78
LARSON, DAN	78	322.2	10	25			151	140	43	7	0	1	4.41
LEE, DON	244	828	40	44			467	281	97	13	4	17	3.61
LEFFERTS, CRAIG	261	385.2	22	22			236	127	5	0	0	17	2.89
LEMAY, DICK	45	107	3	8	139	124	69	49	6	1	0	4	4.21
LEMONDS, DAVE	33	100	4	8			69	43	19	0	0	0	2.97
LEONARD, E. 'DUTCH'	640	3220	191	181			1170	737	375	192	30	44	3.25
LITTLEFIELD, DICK	243	761	33	54			495	413	83	16	0	9	4.72
LOCKER, BOB	576	878	57	39			577	257	0	0	0	95	2.76
LOWN, TURK	504	1031	55	61			574	590	49	10	1	73	4.12
LYNCH, ED	190	829.1	45	45			316	181	111	8	2	4	3.82
MARTIN, MORRIE	250	604	38	34	396	352	245	251	48	8	1	15	4.29
MARTZ, RANDY	68	290.2	17	19			78	100	45	2	0	1	3.78
MASON, MIKE	110	532	25	35			307	195	80	7	2	0	4.31
MAYER, ED	22	32	2	2			17	18	1	0	0	1	4.22
MCDANIEL, LINDY	987	2140	141	119			1361	623	74	18	4	172	3.45
MCGINN, DAN	210	409	15	30			293	225	28	4	2	10	3.98
MCGLOTHEN, LYNN	318	1498	86	93	282	255	939	572	201	41	13	2	3.98
MCLISH, CAL	352	1609	92	92			713	552	209	57	15	6	4.01
MEYER, RUSS	319	1531	94	73			672	541	219	65	13	5	3.99
MIKKELSEN, PETE	364	653	45	40			436	250	3	0	0	49	3.38
MILLER, BOB L.	694	1552	69	81			895	608	99	7	2	52	3.37
MINNER, PAUL	253	1311	69	84			481	393	169	64	9	10	3.94
MOORE, DONNIE	375	596.1	36	36	276	241	377	165	4	3	0	80	3.64
MOREHEAD, SETH	132	316	5	19			184	110	24	3	0	5	4.81
MOSKAU, PAUL	148	634	32	27			374	243	92	7	4	4	4.22
MOYER, JAMIE	16	87.1	7	4	52	49	45	42	16	0	0	0	5.05
NEWMAN, RAY	45	63	3	3			46	24	4	0	0	4	3.00
NEWSOM, BOBO	600	3758	211	222	1506	1331	2082	1732		246	30	21	3.99
NICHOLS, DOLAN	24	41	0	1			16	19	0	0	0	1	3.58
NIEKRO, JOE	670	3426	213	190			1656	1191	472	106	29	16	3.50
NOLES, DICKIE	229	789.2	32	48			421	310	93	3	3	7	4.56
NORMAN, FRED	403	1938	104	103			1303	815	268	56	15	8	3.64
NOTTEBART, DON	296	927	36	51			525	283	89	16	4	21	3.66
NYE, RICH	113	478	26	31			267	140	63	16	4	1	3.71
PAPPAS, MILT	520	3186	209	164			1728	858	465	129	43	4	3.40
PATTERSON, REGGIE	14	31.2	1	4			17	14	4	0	0	0	7.96
PAUL, MIKE	228	627	27	48			452	246	77	5	1	8	3.92
PERKOWSKI, HARRY	184	698	33	40			296	324	76	24	4	6	4.37
PHILLIPS, TAYLOR	147	439	16	22			233	211	45	9	1	6	4.82
PHOEBUS, TOM	201	1030	56	52			725	489	149	29	11	6	3.33
PINA, HORACIO	314	432	23	23			278	216	7	0	0	38	3.25
PIZARRO, JUAN	488	2035	131	105			1520	888	245	79	17	28	3.43
POHOLSKY, TOM	159	754	31	52			316	192	104	30	5	1	3.93
POLLET, HOWIE	403	2106	131	116			934	745	277	116	20	20	3.51
PORTERFIELD, BOB	318	1568	87	97			572	552	193	92	23	8	3.79
PROLY, MIKE	267	546	22	29			185	195	18	0	0	22	3.23
RADATZ, DICK	381	694	52	43			745	296	0	0	0	122	3.13
RAFFENSBERGER, KEN	396	2152	119	154			806	449	292	133	31	16	3.60
RAINEY, CHUCK	141	670	43	35			300	287	106	10	6	1	4.50
RAMSDELL, WILLARD	111	480	24	39			240	215	58	18	0	5	3.83
REBERGER, FRANK	148	389	14	15			258	197	37	5	0	8	4.51
REGAN, PHIL	551	1373	96	81			743	447	105	20	1	92	3.83
RENKO, STEVE	451	2493.1	134	146			1455	1010	365	57	9	6	4.00
REUSCHEL, PAUL	188	393.2	16	16			188	132	1	0	0	13	4.51
REUSCHEL, RICK	436	2771.2	152	155	1195	1056	1652	759	414	81	20	4	3.43
REYNOLDS, ARCHIE	36	81	0	5			47	49	7	0	0	0	5.78
RILEY, GEORGE	31	78.1	1	5			35	33	5	0	0	0	5.06

PLAYER	G	IP	W	L	R	ER	SO	BB	GS	CG	SHO	SV	ERA
RIPLEY, ALLEN	101	464.2	23	27			229	148	67	4	0	1	4.51
ROBERTS, DAVE A.	445	2098	103	125			957	615	277	77	20	15	3.78
ROBERTS, ROBIN	676	4689	286	245			2357	902	609	305	45	25	3.40
RODRIGUEZ, ROBERTO	57	112	3	2			91	37	5	0	0	5	4.82
ROOT, CHARLIE	632	3197	201	160			1459	889	341	177	21	40	3.59
ROSS, GARY	283	713	25	47			378	288	8	2	1	7	3.92
RUSH, BOB	417	2409	127	152			1244	789	321	118	16	8	3.65
RUTHVEN, DICK	349	2098.1	123	127			1142	761	332	61	1	1	4.13
SANDERSON, SCOTT	229	1313.2	78	69	551	497	883	328	207	30	9	3	3.40
SCHAFFERNOTH, JOE	74	118	3	8			68	53	1	0	0	3	4.58
SCHMITZ, JOHNNY	366	1813	93	114			746	757	235	86	16	19	2.97
SCHROLL, AL	35	118	6	9			63	64	13	3	0	3	5.34
SCHULTZ, BARNEY	227	347	20	20			264	116	0	0	0	35	3.63
SCHULTZ, BOB	65	182	9	13			67	125	19	3	0	5	5.19
SCHULTZ, BUDDY	168	240	15	9			193	88	3	0	0	12	3.67
SCHULZE, DON	62	281.2	11	21	191	171	119	88	49	4	0	0	5.46
SCHURR, WAYNE	26	48	0	0			29	11	0	0	0	0	3.75
SELMA, DICK	307	841	42	54			681	328	76	11	6	31	3.62
SHANTZ, BOBBY	537	1936	119	99			880	511	171	78	15	48	3.38
SHAW, BOB	430	1779	108	98			880	511	223	55	15	32	3.52
SIMMONS, CURT	569	3349	193	183			1697	1063	461	163	36	5	3.54
SINGLETON, ELMER	145	327	11	17			160	146	19	2	0	0	4.84
SLAUGHTER, STERLING	20	52	2	4			32	32	6	1	0	0	5.71
SMITH, BOB W.	30	97	4	4			60	59	10	1	0	0	4.73
SMITH, LEE	396	598.1	36	41	210	192	548	232	6	0	0	144	2.89
SOLIS, MARCELINO	15	52	3	3			15	20	4	0	0	0	6.06
SOLOMON, EDDIE	191	718	36	42			337	247	95	8	0	4	4.00
SORENSEN, LARY	311	1671.2	90	99			539	387	230	69	10	3	4.12
SPRING, JACK	155	186	12	5			86	78	5	0	0	8	4.26
STEEVENS, MORRIE	22	21	1	1			11	16	1	0	0	0	4.29
STEN, RANDY	55	133.1	5	6			93	81	8	1	0	1	5.74
STEPHENSON, EARL	54	113	4	5			50	49	8	0	0	1	3.58
STODDARD, TIM	336	560.1	35	30	257	238	459	292	0	0	0	65	3.82
STONE, STEVE	320	1789	107	93			1065	716	269	43	7	1	3.96
STONEMAN, BILL	245	1238	54	84			934	602	170	46	15	5	4.08
SUTCLIFFE, RICK	251	1416.2	86	68	669	605	934	599	191	41	12	5	3.84
SUTTER, BRUCE	623	955.1	67	67	344	304	821	298	0	0	0	286	2.75
TEWKSBURY, BOB	23	130.1	9	5	58	48	49	31	20	2	0	0	3.31
TIDROW, DICK	620	1747	100	94			967	572	138	33	5	55	3.63
TIEFENAUER, BOB	179	316	9	25			204	87	8	0	0	23	3.84
TODD, JIM	270	512	25	23			194	239	8	0	0	24	4.22
TOMPKINS, RON	40	50	0	2			24	54	1	0	0	0	3.96
TOTH, PAUL	43	193	9	12			32	54	21	5	2	0	3.78
TREMEL, BILL	57	91	4	5			34	46	0	0	0	6	4.05
TROUT, STEVE	242	1294	74	75	648	567	536	466	200	29	7	4	3.94
UPHAM, JOHN	7	8.1	0	1			4	5	0	0	0	0	5.63
VALENTINETTI, VITO	108	257	13	14			94	122	15	3	0	10	3.93
WADE, BEN	118	371	19	17			235	181	25	5	1	10	4.34
WARNER, JACK D.	33	55	0	2			23	21	0	0	0	0	5.07
WATT, EDDIE	411	660	38	36			462	254	13	0	0	80	2.90
WILCOX, MILT	381	1958.1	119	105			1111	742	273	73	10	6	4.04
WILHELM, HOYT	1070	2253	143	122			1610	778	52	20	5	227	2.52
WILLIS, JIM	58	83	2	4			20	35	4	2	0	0	3.41
WRIGHT, MEL	27	66	2	2			36		0	0	0	3	7.70
ZAHN, GEOFF	304	1848.2	111	109			705	526	270	79	20	0	3.74
ZAMORA, OSCAR	158	225	13	15			99	60	2	0	0	23	7.16

Batting Record & Index

PLAYER	G	AB	R	H	2B	3B	HR	RBI	SB	SLG	BB	SO	AVG
ADAMS, BOBBY	1281	4019	591	1082	188	49	37	303	67	.368	414	447	.269
ADAMS, MIKE	100	118	27	23	5	0	3	9	2	.314	32	29	.195
ADDIS, BOB	208	534	70	150	22	4	2	47	8	.341	37	47	.281
ALEXANDER, MATT	374	168	111	36	4	2	0	4	103	.262	18	26	.214
ALTMAN, GEORGE	991	3091	409	832	132	34	101	403	52	.432	185	572	.269
AMALFITANO, JOE	643	1715	248	418	67	19	9	123	19	.314	185	224	.244
ARCIA, JOSE	293	615	78	132	24	6	1	35	17	.278	78	107	.215
ASHBURN, RICHIE	2189	8365	1322	2574	317	109	29	586	234	.382	1198	571	.308
ASPROMONTE, KEN	475	1483	171	369	69	7	19	124	7	.338	179	149	.249
ATWELL, TOBY	378	1117	116	290	41	7	9	110	4	.333	161	84	.260
AVERILL, EARL	449	1031	137	249	41	7	44	159	7	.409	162	220	.242
BAILEY, ED	1212	3583	432	915	128	15	155	540	17	.429	545	577	.256
BAKER, GENE	630	2230	265	590	109	21	39	227	21	.385	184	219	.265
BANKS, ERNIE	2528	9421	1305	2583	407	90	512	1636	50	.500	763	1236	.274
BARRAGAN, CUNO	69	163	14	33	6	1	3	14	0	.270	23	36	.202
BAUMHOLTZ, FRANK	1019	3477	450	1010	165	51	25	272	30	.389	258	258	.290
BECKERT, GLENN	1320	5208	685	1473	196	31	22	360	49	.341	260	243	.283
BERTELL, DICK	444	1310	91	327	34	9	10	112	2	.312	106	188	.250
BITTNER, LARRY	1217	3151	310	861	144	20	58	354	9	.362	236	287	.273
BILKO, STEVE	600	1738	220	432	85	13	76	276	2	.444	234	395	.249
BLACKWELL, TIM	426	1044	91	238	40	11	6	80	6	.305	154	183	.228
BLADT, RICH	62	130	14	28	3	1	1	12	6	.277	11	13	.215
BOBB, RANDY	10	10	0	1	0	0	0	0	0	.100	1	3	.100
BOCCABELLA, JOHN	551	1462	117	320	56	5	26	148	3	.317	96	246	.219
BOLGER, JIM	312	612	65	140	14	6	6	48	3	.301	32	83	.229
BONDS, BOBBY	1849	7043	1258	1886	302	66	332	1024	461	.471	914	1757	.268
BORKOWSKI, BOB	470	1170	126	294	43	10	16	112	4	.346	76	166	.251
BOROS, STEVE	422	1255	141	308	50	7	26	149	11	.359	181	174	.245
BOSLEY, THAD	587	1276	152	353	37	11	17	121	43	.363	119	213	.277
BOUCHEE, ED	670	2199	298	583	114	21	61	290	1	.419	340	401	.265
BOURQUE, PAT	201	405	36	87	17	2	17	61	2	.356	58	73	.215
BOWA, LARRY	2161	8204	972	2141	255	95	15	510	461	.321	461	547	.261
BREEDEN, DANNY	28	73	3	11	1	0	2	5	0	.164	9	21	.151
BREEDEN, HAL	273	608	61	148	28	6	21	76	0	.413	69	107	.243
BRIGGS, DAN	325	688	67	134	20	6	12	53	2	.294	45	133	.195
BRIGHT, HARRY	336	839	94	214	31	4	32	126	2	.416	65	133	.255
BROCK, LOU	2616	10332	1610	3023	486	141	149	900	938	.410	761	1730	.293
BROWN, TOMMY M.	494	1280	151	309	39	7	31	159	7	.355	85	142	.241
BROWNE, BYRON	59	109	6	24	3	1	2	13	1	.275	6	25	.220
BRYANT, DON	349	869	94	205	37	0	10	102	1	.236	25	273	.236
BUCKNER, BILL	2176	8424	1008	2464	462	46	164	1072	175	.446	402	395	.292
BURGESS, SMOKY	1691	4471	485	1318	230	33	126	673	13	.417	477	270	.295
BURKE, LEO	165	301	33	72	9	4	17	45	0	.365	21	79	.239
BURTON, ELLIS	215	556	79	120	24	4	17	59	11	.365	65	117	.216
CALLISON, JOHNNY	1886	6652	926	1757	321	89	226	840	74	.441	650	1064	.264
CAMPBELL, RON	52	154	11	38	7	1	1	14	1	.325	7	26	.247
CANNIZZARO, CHRIS	740	1950	132	458	66	1	18	169	3	.309	241	354	.235
CARDENAL, JOSE	2017	6964	936	1913	333	46	138	775	329	.395	608	807	.275
CARTER, JOE	394	1447	210	404	70	11	57	222	56	.461	68	238	.279
CARTY, RICO	1651	5606	712	1677	278	17	204	890	21	.464	642	663	.299
CAVARRETTA, PHIL	2030	6754	990	1977	347	99	95	920	65	.416	820	598	.293
CEY, RON	2028	7058	965	1845	322	21	312	1128	24	.446	990	1203	.261
CHITI, HARRY	502	1495	135	356	49	9	41	179	4	.365	115	242	.238
CLEMENS, DOUG	452	920	99	211	34	7	12	88	6	.321	114	166	.229
CLINE, TY	892	1834	251	437	53	25	12	125	22	.304	153	262	.238
CLINES, GENE	870	2328	314	645	85	24	5	187	71	.341	169	271	.277
COGGINS, FRANK	87	247	25	53	9	1	1	15	2	.271	12	50	.215
COOPER, WALKER	1473	4702	573	1341	240	40	173	812	18	.464	309	357	.285
COTTO, HENRY	174	282	39	74	9	0	2	20	13	.316	15	52	.262
COVINGTON, WES	1075	2978	355	832	128	17	131	499	7	.466	247	414	.279
COWAN, BILLY	493	1190	131	281	44	8	40	125	17	.387	70	297	.236
COX, LARRY	348	825	72	182	31	5	12	85	5	.314	70	117	.221
CRUZ, HECTOR	624	1607	186	361	71	9	39	200	5	.353	175	314	.225
DARK, ALVIN	1828	7219	1064	2089	358	72	126	757	59	.411	430	534	.289
DARWIN, BOBBY	646	2224	250	559	76	16	83	328	16	.412	160	577	.251
DAVIS, BROCK	243	543	46	141	12	5	1	43	7	.306	57	73	.260
DAVIS, JODY	777	2641	274	671	138	6	97	383	6	.423	226	505	.254
DAVIS, TOMMY	1999	7223	811	2121	272	35	153	1052	136	.405	381	754	.294
DAWSON, ANDRE	1443	5628	828	1575	295	67	225	838	253	.476	354	896	.280
DAY, BOOTS	471	1151	146	295	28	6	8	98	15	.312	95	141	.256
DAYETT, BRIAN	121	249	25	61	12	1	9	43	0	.410	17	34	.245
DEJESUS, IVAN	1348	4571	593	1162	175	48	21	323	194	.327	464	657	.254
DEL GRECO, BOBBY	731	1982	271	454	95	11	42	169	16	.352	372	372	.229
DERNIER, BOB	636	1931	291	491	80	11	13	108	185	.327	180	235	.254
DIAZ, MIKE	103	216	24	58	10	2	13	37	0	.481	15	43	.269
DILLARD, STEVE	438	1013	148	246	50	6	13	102	15	.343	76	147	.243
DILONE, MIGUEL	722	1870	296	504	67	22	6	122	250	.339	132	178	.270
DRAKE, SAMMY	53	72	8	11	0	0	1	2	1	.153	8	17	.153
DRAKE, SOLLY	141	285	41	66	10	7	2	18	15	.295	32	53	.232
DUNSTON, SHAWON	224	831	106	210	48	7	26	86	24	.403	40	156	.253
DURHAM, LEON	862	3006	436	844	160	38	116	458	104	.475	377	551	.281
DUROCHER, LEO	1637	5350	575	1320	210	56	24	567	31	.320	377	480	.247
EDWARDS, BRUCE	591	1675	191	429	67	20	39	241	9	.390	190	179	.256
EDWARDS, HANK	735	2191	285	613	116	41	51	276	9	.440	208	264	.280
ELIA, LEE	95	212	17	43	5	2	3	25	0	.288	15	45	.203
FANZONE, CARMEN	237	588	66	132	27	5	20	94	3	.372	74	119	.224
FELSKE, JOHN	54	104	7	14	3	1	1	9	0	.212	9	35	.135
FERNANDEZ, FRAN	285	727	92	145	21	1	39	116	2	.395	164	231	.199
FIGUEROA, JESUS	115	196	20	50	5	0	1	11	14	.293	14	16	.253
FLETCHER, SCOTT	559	1619	218	426	75	14	11	149	33	.347	163	183	.263
FONDY, DEE	967	3502	437	1000	144	47	69	373	84	.413	203	526	.286
FOOTE, BARRY	687	2127	191	489	103	10	57	230	10	.368	136	287	.230
FRANCONA, TERRY	451	1075	96	307	51	8	16	96	8	.367	42	69	.286
FRANKS, HERMAN	188	403	35	80	18	2	3	43	2	.275	57	37	.199
FRIEND, OWEN	208	598	69	136	24		13	76	2	.339	55	109	.227
GABRIELSON, LEN	708	1764	176	446	64	12	37	176	20	.366	145	315	.253
GAGLIANO, PHIL	702	1411	150	336	50	7	14	159	5	.313	163	184	.238
GALAN, AUGIE	1742	5937	1004	1706	337	74	100	830	123	.419	979	393	.287
GAMBLE, OSCAR	1584	4502	656	1195	188	31	200	666	47	.454	610	546	.265
GARAGIOLA, JOE	676	1873	198	481	82	16	42	255	5	.385	267	173	.257
GARRETT, ADRIAN	163	276	30	51	8	0	11	37	4	.333	31	87	.185
GERNERT, DICK	835	2493	357	632	104	2	103	402	10	.426	363	462	.254
GIGON, NORM	34	70	8	12	3	1	1	6	0	.286		14	.171
GOMEZ, PRESTON	8	7	2	2	1			1	0	.429		4	.286
GORYL, JOHN	276	595	79	134	19	10	16	48	2	.371	64	106	.225
GRABARKEWITZ, BILLY	466	1161	189	274	41	12	28	141	33	.364	202	321	.236
GRAMMAS, ALEX	913	2073	236	512	90	10	12	163	17	.317	206	193	.247
GRIMM, CHARLIE	2164	7917	908	2299	394	108	79	1078	57	.397	410		.290
GROSS, GREG	1537	3404	423	993	125	45	6	287	39	.360	578	229	.292
HAAS, EDDIE	55	70	9	17	3	0	0	10	0	.329	8	20	.243
HACK, STAN	1938	7278	1239	2193	363	81	57	642	165	.397	1092	466	.301
HALL, JIMMIE	968	2848	387	724	100	24	121	391	38	.434	287	529	.254